Artists for Conservation

2016

International Exhibit of Nature in Art

Artists for Conservation's annual exhibit celebrates artistic excellence in the depiction of nature, raises awareness of important conservation issues and directly supports organizations dedicated to addressing them.

Artists for Conservation

— 2016 —

International Exhibit of Nature in Art

www.ArtistsForConservation.org

Artists for Conservation's annual exhibit of the Artists for Conservation Foundation—the world's leading artist group supporting the environment.

Published by the Artists for Conservation Foundation

Introduction by:
Jeffrey Whiting

This book has been published as a companion to the Artists for Conservation 2016 Exhibit, produced by the Artists for Conservation Foundation.

AFC would like to express its gratitude to RE/MAX for supporting the 2016 Artists for Conservation Festival and art exhibit.

Table of Contents

Photo by Yasaman Whiting

Introduction

by Jeffrey Whiting,
President and Founder, Artists for Conservation

Every fall since 2008 has been a special time, when artists from around the globe convene at Artists for Conservation's exhibit premiere, to share their knowledge, passion, expertise and camaraderie. Many donate their time to offer public presentations, workshops, live demonstrations and more. Each brings a unique perspective through their paintings and sculptures, and a deep understanding and reverence for the subjects they portray. These artists are a part of a very special international AFC community that has grown over nearly two decades and spanning almost 30 countries.

The world has changed significantly since our humble beginnings as an online community in the first few years after the birth of the Web. Watch any given news program, and it can easily feel more challenging than ever to be advocating for support of species conservation, in a world that seems to be increasingly violent, divided, extremist, protectionist and politically and economically unstable.

The threats society faces today are real, but also divert needed attention from responsible stewardship and maintaining the aim toward a sustainable and diverse future. They threaten to thwart our exploring the great diversity of our planet. Albert Einstein once said, "Peace cannot be kept by force. It can only be achieved by understanding."

With so many existential priorities vying for our attention, there is one salient message that we, as "conservation communicators", must work to remind society: that the diversity of life around us is our life support as a species. Capturing in art what we have in our world and striving to make big strides in conservation are more important than ever. Our youth hopefully will continue to have the opportunities to travel and experience the natural and cultural wonders around the world as recent generations have enjoyed.

As artists supporting AFC's mission, we are equally susceptible to the effects of depressing news as anyone, but we remain committed to supporting the conservation movement, educating and supporting youth, and recognizing those in our community who go beyond the call of duty in this regard. I'm inspired by the artist community like no other, at their optimism and passion for protecting what's left of our natural heritage, both for its beauty and its life-giving resources.

To that end, it's with great pride that we honor another long-time member and master artist, Guy Coheleach, with the Simon Combes Conservation Award. We're also thrilled to welcome in-ternational art and conservation icon, Robert Bateman, back as our Festival Patron for a fourth time.

This is an exciting time for the organization overall. We recently launched a new Festival website, and AFC artists are in the process of transitioning to a next-generation format that is highly mobile and social media friendly. We are using this technology boost to enable new initiatives such as a collaborative mosaic super-mural depicting over 600 of the world's endangered species of birds, a photographic competition, and a new mentorship program. The mentorship program is designed to support the artistic development of our current artist members as well as embrace and inspire other emerging artists to join and support our movement to foster conservation through art worldwide.

We're continuing to develop new partnerships and strengthening existing ones, with organizations such as the International Ornithological Congress 2018, the Arizona-Sonora Desert Museum and the establishment of two new awards with Arabella Magazine and the Desert Museum. These opportunities are exciting for our artists, as well as for those appreciating the art that has been created for this exhibit and to support the species and places depicted.

At the heart of this book is the extraordinary exhibit it showcases along with the talents of artists from 15 countries. The AFC exhibit is unique – our exhibits and programs are designed to both raise awareness and support fundraising for a multitude of organizations, aside from AFC, who are doing the difficult conservation work in the field. Each artwork is dedicated by the artist to a conservation cause of the artist's choosing. Each year, the exhibit is used as an instructional tool for hundreds of students.

I sincerely hope that you can join us in Vancouver or in Tucson, Arizona, or elsewhere for live exhibits of many of the works in this book. For the many reading this who live far away from either location, I invite you to enjoy the pages of this book and AFC's online home at www.ArtistsForConservation.org and on social media, where the world can be frighteningly, but also beautifully small.

In closing, I'd like to thank the dozens of volunteers, artists and art-admirers alike who help bring our exhibit and festival programs to fruition each year… and to you, our supporters who have found inspiration in "the art of conservation".

Jeffrey Whiting, AFC President & Founder

The Exhibit

The Art of Conservation exhibition celebrates artistic excellence in the depiction of nature, raises awareness of important conservation issues and directly supports organizations dedicated to addressing them.

2016 Judges

The AFC extends its sincere thanks to the following individuals who served as the jury panel for the selection of the artworks included in this show.

- Brent Cooke (Canada) AFC Signature Member (Sculptor) and Board Member;

- Michael Dumas (Canada), AFC Signature Member (Painter);

- Pollyanna Pickering (UK) AFC Signature Member (Painter) & Simon Combes Award Recipient;

- Holly Swangstu (USA) Art Institute Director, Arizona-Sonora Desert Museum;

- Debra Usher (Canada) Publisher & Editor in Chief, Arabella Magazine.

2016 Award Winners

Medals of Excellence

- Douglas Aja for his sculpture, *"Football Buddies"*;

- Stephane Alsac for his painting, *"Bad Lieutenant"*;

- Julia Hargreaves for her painting, "Bird Bath";

- Hans Kappel for his painting, *"Sleeping Fennec"*;

- David Kitler for his painting, *"Piece Keepers"*;

- Bruce Lawes for his painting, "Savannah Siesta";

- Bruce Lawes for his painting, *"All Tucked In"*;

- Leo Osborne for his painting, *"Return to Turtle Island"*, and

- Rosetta for her sculpture, *"Awakening Pride"*.

Best-in-Show

- David Kitler for his painting, *"Piece Keepers"*, and

- Rosetta for her sculpture, *"Awakening Pride"*.

Environmental Statement Award

- David Kitler for his painting, *"Piece Keepers"*

Exhibiting Artists

Following is a list of all artists whose artwork is represented in the Artists for Conservation 2016 exhibit. As with the list, the artworks featured on the pages that follow appear in alphabetical order of the artists' names.

Aja, Douglas (USA)
Alleman, Carol (USA)
Alsac, Stephane (France)
Armstrong, Rosemarie (Canada)
Arnett, Stuart (Canada)
Bach, Del-Bourree (USA)
Ballantyne, Sheila (Canada)
Banks, Patricia (Canada)
Banovich, John (USA)
Besse, Linda (USA)
Billingsley, Cindy (USA)
Bork, Beatrice (USA)
Branson, Lynn (Canada)
Breger, Varda (Israel)
Brest van Kempen, Carel (USA)
Bruynzeel, Renata (Australia)
Cadène, Florence (France)
Cogley, Elizabeth (Australia)
Cook, Carrie (USA)
Cooke, Brent (Canada)
Crouter, Anni (USA)
Crowe, Becci (USA)
Curry, Dennis (USA)
deKramer, Karyn (USA)
Dodge, Kelly (Canada)
Dreelinck, Tania (Belgium)
Dreyer, Rob (USA)
Duffek, Kim (USA)
Dumas, Michael (Canada)
Dunn, Kathleen (USA)
Dunphy, Kathleen (USA)
DuPuis-Rosen, Linda (USA)
Erikson, Lynn (Canada)
Feltner, Linda (USA)
Fiorentino, James (USA)
Fisher, Cynthie (USA)
Gallup, David (USA)
Gates, Martin (USA)
Goulding, Fiona (New Zealand)
Gray, Peter (South Africa)
Griffin, Patricia (USA)
Hallett, Mark (USA)
Hamanaka, Setsuo (Japan)
Hargreaves, Julia (Canada)
Harvey, Guy (Cayman Islands)
Haycock, Kathy (Canada)
Heaton, Janet (USA)
Hobson, Mark (Canada)

Hough, James (Australia)
Hughbanks, Debbie (USA)
Isaac, Terry (Canada)
Ivanyi, Rachel (USA)
Jackman, Pat (USA)
Jenvey, Kate (Australia)
Jesic, Stephen (Australia)
Jessen, Mary Jane (Canada)
Kappel, Hans (Germany)
Karryl, (USA)
Katrandzhiev, Valentin (Bulgaria)
Kiesow, James (USA)
Kissinger, Megan (USA)
Kitler, David (Canada)
Koensgen, Joseph (Canada)
Koller, Rebecca (Australia)
Kopeschny, Barbara (Canada)
Krishnan, Krish (USA)
LaFogg-Docherty, Deborah (USA)
Laurence-Rowe, Karen (Kenya)
Lawes, Bruce (Canada)
Lindamood, Patsy (USA)
Lingham, Steven (Australia)
Lutz, Jan (USA)
Mansell, Patricia (Canada)
Marshall, Pete (Australia)
Maynard, Chris (USA)
McClelland, Chris (Australia)
McCune, Michelle (USA)
McManiman, Candy (Canada)
McMillan, Vickie (USA)
Megahan, John (USA)
Milligan, Billy-Jack (Canada)
Millington, Marti (USA)
Morvell, Steve (Australia)
Munkittrick, Dianne (USA)
Murray, Robin (USA)
Nicholls, Calvin (Canada)
Nordwall, Solveig (USA)
Norwich-Young, Dorset (Canada)
Orlando, Ron (USA)
Osborne, Leo (USA)
O'Sullivan, Mary Louise (USA)
Parsons, Victoria (USA)
Peyton, Anne (USA)
Phillips, Murray (Canada)
Pickering, Pollyanna (UK)
Plaizier, Ron (Canada)

Pratt, Heidi (USA)
Prescott, David (USA)
Qiu, Ji (Australia)
Raffield, Natalie (USA)
Rankin, David (USA)
Rich, Andrea (USA)
Richman, Rebecca (USA)
Roberts, Craig (UK)
Rogers, Valerie (Canada)
Rosetta, (USA)
Rossin, Linda (USA)
Rusin, Len (USA)
Saenz, Eleazar (Mexico)
Schafer, Sharon K. (USA)
Schlenker, Robert (USA)
Scott, Nathan (Canada)
Seerey-Lester, John (USA)
Seerey-Lester, Suzie (USA)
Simmons, Geraldine (Australia)
Snoots, Karin (USA)
Solberg, Morten (USA)
Sorley-Keichinger, Cindy (Canada)
Sowden, Peggy (Canada)
Spera, Edward (Canada)
Stewart, James (Canada)
Strelive, Uta (Canada)
Studwell, Judy (USA)
Susinno, Mark (USA)
Sutton, Linda (USA)
Taylor, Mary (USA)
Theriault, Colette (Canada)
Thompson, Martha (USA)
Tiessen, Josh (Canada)
Toft, Kim (Australia)
Truss, Jonathan (UK)
Trygg, Joyce (Canada)
Van Rijn, Eva (USA)
Venditti, Jerry (USA)
Vik, Lyn (Canada)
Walsh, Frank (USA)
Watanabe, Yasuo (Japan)
Wheeler, Rick (USA)
Whiting, Jeffrey (Canada)
Wiegmink, Paula (Australia)
Winters, Ria (The Netherlands)
Woodall, Terry (USA)

DOUGLAS AJA (USA)

Football Buddies
Orphaned African elephant with keeper
Bronze
13" x 16" x 10"

"'Football Buddies' depicts an orphaned elephant calf and keeper chasing after a soccer ball. The keeper is Edwin Lusichi, Project Manager - Nairobi Orphan Nursery of the David Sheldrick Wildlife Trust (DSWT) in Nairobi, Kenya. Calves are orphaned for many reasons, mostly because of poaching to feed the illegal ivory trade. The fortunate ones are brought to the DSWT where they are cared for and eventually reintroduced into the wild, a process that takes many years. The calves' days are spent playing and exploring the bush, always watched over by the keepers."

DOUGLAS AJA (USA)

Thirsty Warthog (2015)
Warthog, Red-billed Oxpecker
Bronze
9" x 13" x 7.5"

"Warthogs are omnivores and the only pig species adapted to grazing and living in savanna habitats. While feeding, they usually bend their front feet backwards and move around on their wrists. They have calloused pads on their wrists that protect them from injury. This technique is also used when drinking. This warthog has a red-billed oxpecker on his back. The oxpecker helps relieve the warthog of parasites by eating ticks and other bloodsucking insects."

CAROL ALLEMAN (USA)

Love Blooms
Wild Violet Plant
Bronze
8.5" x 4.75" x 4.75"

"The wild violet stems flexibly bend, inviting us to notice the graceful beauty of flexibility as we too grow. Rising from their heart-shaped leaves, they dance a quiet, lovely ballet for us.

Three ants are etched on the bottom of the vessel (hidden). Drawn to the oils in the seeds, ants literally farm the seeds underground, a process called myrmecochory. The shell is too hard for them to eat thus the seeds are both scattered and protected from birds and rodents, allowing them greater chance of germination. How often do we neglect to be grateful for the many 'invisible helpers' in our lives? They are ever present working on our behalf, while often invisible to us.

With its 37 blooms it invites us to notice our invisible helpers, and the rich gifts of modesty and flexibility, within a blanket of love. Companion writings accompany my sculptures."

STEPHANE ALSAC (FRANCE)

Bad Lieutenant
Wild Boar
Oil
47" x 27"

" '*Bad Lieutenant*' is the representation of the personality of the old boar: changeable and unpredictable. The European Wild Boar is a courageous, fearless animal with a high sense of sociability.

This piece of art has been made to pay tribute to this."

STEPHANE ALSAC (FRANCE)

Elephant Portrait
Elephant
Oil
59" x 28"

"Do not try to intimidate an elephant! He's the best at this game.
A young adult elephant can act high and mighty, but you should understand the first warning and not play with fire. "

ROSEMARIE ARMSTRONG
(CANADA)

Solitude
Seascape
Oil on canvas
24" x 48"

"This panoramic seascape was inspired by my explorations of MacKenzie Beach and Chesterman Beach, Vancouver Island. Here the rocky outcroppings create an other-worldly feeling when the mists roll in from the sea. When the tide is out, there are a great many geographical features and sea life to discover."

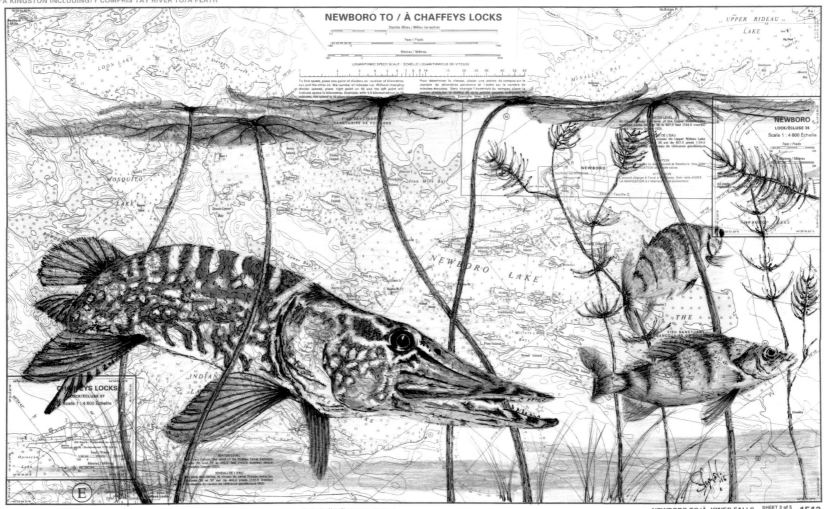

STUART ARNETT (CANADA)

The Chase
Northern Pike and Yellow Perch
Graphite and Staedtler Marker
14.5" x 22"

"This is a true mixed media piece. I call them '*artistic cartography*' - graphite and Staedtler marker on a nautical chart of the Rideau Lakes in Eastern Ontario. Northern Pike, sometimes nicknamed the 'Water Wolf', always venture into the shallows in the early evening to hunt for perch and other feeder fish. This is why perch tend to stay in schools so that when they try to escape and dart in different directions the predator gets confused and is not sure which one to pursue. The chase is on!"

STUART ARNETT (CANADA)

Horseshoe Beach

Red Knots, Ruddy Turnstones and Horseshoe Crabs
Graphite

"'Horseshoe Beach' was one of my largest projects – a total of 12 shorebirds, 9 Red Knots and 3 Ruddy Turnstones. The Red Knot is a magnificent little bird that is endangered due to the over fishing of the Horseshoe Crab. The Red Knot flies from Argentina where it winters to Delaware Bay where it feeds on Horseshoe Crab eggs and once replenished with nourishment flies to the Canadian Arctic where it raises its young. Without the Horseshoe Crab it would not survive the trip to the Arctic."

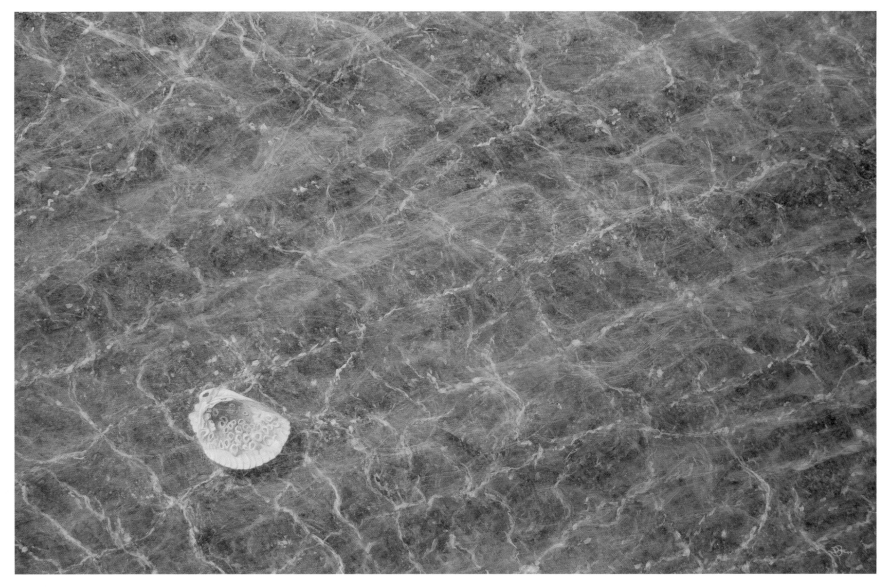

DEL-BOURREE BACH (USA)

Barnacle Bill
Cockle shell with barnacles in the shallows
Acrylic on panel
24" x 36"

"In the shallow waters and on the beaches of Florida's Gulf Coast, beautiful shells abound, the remains of a multitude of species. Although the cockle shell's original inhabitant is long gone, the cycle of life continues as barnacles make it their home. "

DEL-BOURREE BACH (USA)

First Snow
Great Blue Heron wintering over on Cape Cod
Acrylic on panel
12" x 19"

"This Great Blue Heron has decided, as quite a number of them are doing, to winter over on Cape Cod. He's flying over the Oyster River in Chatham in early winter after the first snow. It is a beautiful sight and throughout the winter months he was often seen feeding in the shallow waters there and sitting in the trees along the bluff."

SHEILA BALLANTYNE (CANADA)

Majestic
Lake scene with loon
Acrylic on canvas
40" x 60"

"Art is a means of expression and in this piece my intent was to capture a sublime moment in time - majestic beauty, brought forth by the Creator's hand."

PATRICIA BANKS
(CANADA)

Nurturing
Temperate rainforest landscape
Acrylic on canvas
16" x 12"

"Inspiration comes easily when hiking through nature's tranquil scenery. I am constantly filled with awe and wonder when outdoors in the natural environment and always find new challenges to paint. This scene, though artistically composed, could be anywhere in the rainforests of the Pacific Northwest or in many other places on our beautiful planet. Here, a 'nurse stump' provides nourishment and support to tender young Hemlock trees, which may someday become giants of their species."

**JOHN BANOVICH
(USA)**

Debt Collector
Cape Buffalo
Oil on Belgian linen
28" x 30"

"The old adage that says an elephant never forgets would be matched by a buffalo never forgives. They have been known to attack people that have harmed them many years prior. There is nothing like the total disdain the cape buffalo has for you, clearly conveyed in his stare. Four times stronger than an ox, capable of killing lions, and weighing in at nearly a ton of wild dynamite, the cape buffalo kills more hunters in Africa than any other animal. They say he never forgets and in the words of famed author Robert Rurak, 'The cape buffalo looks at you as If you owe him money' and this is one Debt Collector you never want to come face to face with!"

JOHN BANOVICH (USA)

Red Dawn
Leopard
Oil on Belgian linen
68" x 62"

"Africa boasts the most dramatic sunrises on the planet. Here the red sun rises in the distance. The night had been generous...the sign of a successful hunt lies at his feet. Here in the safety of the tree this male leopard is safe from lions or hyenas stealing his kill, but he must remain vigilant as this area has many cattle and with cattle come people. He will eat and then sleep in the cool shade of the Acacia branches."

LINDA BESSE (USA)

Someone to Watch Over Me
Helmeted guineafowl and lion
Oil
14" x 22"

"For our lunch break, our guide pulled up next to a large Kopje in the Serengeti. It took a couple of seconds before I saw a pair of lionesses on a large rock and a single lioness sleeping in the shade. We weren't the only ones watching the lions, as among the rocks were five helmeted guineafowl. In working out the composition, only three of the birds 'made the cut'. Guineafowl are known for their protective nature and while they wouldn't necessarily be guarding a lion, the title is a hint of their character."

CINDY BILLINGSLEY (USA)

Bees

Honeybees
Various organisms in habitat
Oil
16" x 20"

"A third of our food sources are pollinated by bees. Numerous bee colonies have been lost in recent years. I wanted to show their true beauty and their fascinating body design, and also wanted rich colors to remind you of the goodness of honey."

CINDY BILLINGSLEY (USA)

Fighting Lions
African Lions
Clay
10" x 17" x 18"

"During mating, the male lion will bite the nape of the neck of the female, and the act often ends with the female snarling with bared teeth at the male. Lions are vulnerable to extinction, with a projection of 50 percent loss of their populations over the next 20 years."

BEATRICE BORK (USA)

Glimmer
Copper-rumped Hummingbird
Watercolor and gouache
9.75" x 16"

"I am constantly inspired by the wonders of Trinidad and Tobago, and the intricacies of the ecosystem; there is life upon life in the rainforest. The title 'Glimmer' refers not only to the wonderful reflection of light by the hummingbird, but also to a symbol of hope."

LYNN BRANSON (CANADA)

The Burl That Wanted to be a Bittern
Bittern
Cedar
14" x 12" x 10"

"The natural form of the burl depicted a bittern which was carved from a single piece of Red Cedar. Beautiful grain."

LYNN BRANSON (CANADA)

Cresting the Wave
Kingfisher
Oak
24″ x 22″ x 16″

"This piece of Garry Oak has exceptional grain and colour. The white, representing foam, is the natural color in the wood. The kingfisher has lifted off in his magical form, emerging from the wave."

VARDA BREGER (ISRAEL)

Rhinoman
Rhinoceros
Mixed media on paper
28" x 20"

"My belief is that all the inhabitants of our unique planet are parts of a chain, linked together, and dependent on each other, including all varieties of wildlife and plants. We humans have the task of sharing the planet's resources between us peacefully in order to preserve them for the generations to come. In my paintings and poems, I want to warn against the inherent dangers, while arousing feelings of wonder on the one hand and anxiety on the other hand. Wandering birds, helping each other while flying, are for me a model of a hard way of living in peace, without discrimination of gender, religion, race or nationality. I convey my personal philosophy and feelings also in haiku style poems, following are three of them:

Civilization.
Ignoring the elegies of mother earth.
Flying with your feathers,
Leonardo, flying
beside you, Isaiah,
above a dark abyss,
no bloody borders,
passing over time
to the End of Days
to touch Peace.

If only, if only
I had the wings of a bird
I might from a green tree-top
see peace."

AVIBUS IRATUS

CAREL BREST VAN KEMPEN (USA)

Angry Birds
House Sparrow
Acrylic
16" x 20"

"The process of painting is a series of decisions. In this case, most of those decisions were made completely randomly. I started with the frame, House Sparrow and vine, which were designed in the normal manner, and a list of recently extinct and critically endangered American bird species. I then created a series of chance games to make the other decisions for me: the layout of tiles, the various subject positions and placements, and the colors they're painted. The painting process was fun, progressing towards a completely unknown destination. The birds on the tiles are, from upper left: Ivory-billed Woodpecker, Kaui Akialoa, Southwestern Willow Flycatcher, Great Auk, Labrador Duck, Hawaiian Duck, Carolina Parakeet, Heath Hen, Snail Kite, Passenger Pigeon, Short-tailed Albatross, Ashy Storm-petrel, Gunnison Sage Grouse, Eskimo Curlew, Florida Jay, Masked Bobwhite, Whooping Crane, Hawaiian Crow, Marbled Murrelet, Laysan Teal, California Condor, Golden-cheeked Warbler."

CAREL BREST VAN KEMPEN (USA)

Only While Supplies Last!
Common Starlings, House Mouse
Acrylic
20" x 16"

"Advertisements are designed to catch the eye, but their absolute ubiquity in America makes us disregard them. This visual dissonance made me want to try using them as compositional elements in a painting. Other subjects here include common starlings and a house mouse, not to mention depictions of 34 of the 4,833 animal and plant species deemed critically endangered by the IUCN."

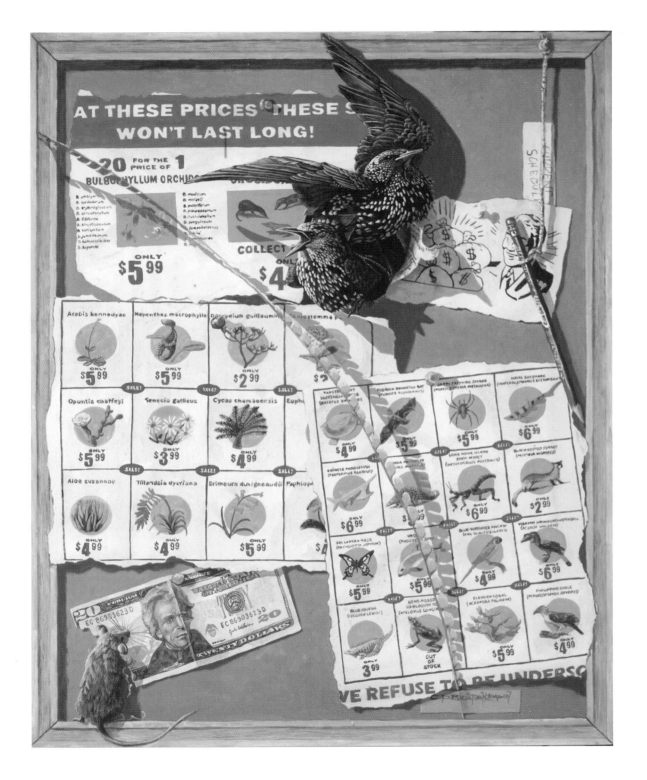

RENATA BRUYNZEEL (AUSTRALIA)

Let's Play - Humpback Whale Calf
Humpback Whale
Pastel
35" x 58"

"I acquired the inspiration for this humpback whale calf pastel from numerous trips I have taken to Vava'u, Tonga, where you can actually go snorkeling with these magnificent creatures.

The whale population in Tonga was severely decimated back in the whaling days and has taken a long while to get back to what it was, so it's great to see the mother and calf population slowly increasing each year and even better to be able to get up close to them."

RENATA BRUYNZEEL (AUSTRALIA)

Green Turtle
Turtle
Pastel
26" x 43"

"I was recently a volunteer helping out with turtle research on Lady Musgrave Island, which is on the southern end of the Great Barrier Reef of Australia.

We were tagging Green and Loggerhead Turtle females after they had laid their eggs on the beach. The tags help keep track of where and when the females come back to lay in the following years. This was an amazing experience and just goes to show how little we know about these amazing creatures."

FLORENCE CADENE (FRANCE)

A Mara Family Winter Tale
Zebras
Charcoal and oil on linen canvas
26″ x 20″

"This is an emotional record of my last visit to Masaï Mara, Kenya where animal species sometimes seem to try offering us the best of our own behaviors."

ELIZABETH COGLEY
(AUSTRALIA)

Eastern Barred Bandicoots
Endangered Species - Eastern
Barred Bandicoots
Mixed medium
14" x 20"

"The Eastern Barred Bandicoot was considered extinct on the mainland of Australia. However, some have recently been discovered in Hamilton, Victoria, sheltering under car wreckage in a tip. Zoos Victoria coordinates a captive breeding program and works closely with the recovery team, to bring the species back from the brink.

The Eastern Barred Bandicoots, in this painting, are from Tasmania, where they are listed as 'requiring monitoring' on the Tasmanian Threatened Species List 1995. Nationally, the Eastern Barred Bandicoot is classified as vulnerable. So far it is believed that foxes have not reached Tasmania and they are working hard to keep it this way. Another threat to the bandicoot is loss of habitat, which is critical to any creature's survival and so it is important for me to include habitat in my work. Also, I do love to paint it."

CARRIE COOK (USA)

The Cost of Palm Oil
Sumatran Orangutan
Oil on canvas
24" x 24"

"Sumatran Orangutans are known for their high intelligence and gentle nature. Because of habitat destruction (mainly due to the farming of palms for palm oil), less than 8,000 remain in the wild. The IUCN lists them as critically endangered."

CARRIE COOK (USA)

Straight Outta Madagascar
Ring-tailed Lemur
Oil on canvas
36" x 12"

"If only I'd traveled to Madagascar to photograph this ring-tailed lemur. In truth, I've never been to Madagascar (neither, I'm sure, has this particular lemur). She resides in the Dallas Zoo, where I was once the graphic design manager. I'm no longer a zoo fan, nor, apparently, were the lemurs, who were notorious escapees.

Wild lemurs may be faring no better, however. Due to destruction of habitat from farming and human overpopulation, Madagascar has less than 10% of its original forest remaining."

BRENT COOKE
(CANADA)

Underwater Waltz
French Angelfish
Stainless steel/bronze/black granite
base
23" x 19" x 19"

"While diving on Grand Cayman
Island, I was fascinated watching two
French angels circling each other for
quite a long time. When I got home
I had to capture the moment in this
sculpture."

ANNI CROUTER (USA)

Spooked
Barred Owl
Watercolor
11" x 15"

"As we were walking through a bird refuge in New York State we came across a large group of barred owls. The public did not visit often so when they saw us they all puffed up and clicked their beaks, therefore the name '*Spooked*'."

ANNI CROUTER (USA)

Waiting on Wonderland
Snowshoe Hare
Watercolor
12" x 24"

"On a late August morning, driving up into the mountains of Colorado, we saw many snowshoe hares. They were just beginning to show hints of white fur, turning for winter."

BECCI CROWE (USA)

Arthur
Adult Male Mandrill
Pen and colored inks
17" x 11"

"I was awestruck as I watched this adult male mandrill in the rainforest of the Republic of Congo. His furry head crest, full mane, blue ridges surrounding a red nose and lips, and golden beard made him appear unworldly. Mandrills are the largest of all monkeys. Living in the rainforests of equatorial Africa, they are shy and reclusive and much remains unknown about these colorful primates. Hunted as bush meat and threatened by a shrinking rainforest their future survival is in question. I created this portrait of Arthur as part of a Congo series to raise awareness about the plight of this spectacular species."

DENNIS CURRY
(USA)

A Touch of Light
Landscape
Oil
24" x 18"

"A touch of light momentarily illuminates this buttress at the base of Yosemite's famous Half Dome. This painting was awarded second place honors at the *2015 Yosemite Renaissance XXX* exhibit held at the Yosemite Museum Gallery."

KARYN DEKRAMER (USA)

Young Beaver

North American Beaver
Watercolor
11" x 30"

"A young beaver drifts, chomping on a sprig of aspen and fattening himself up for the harsh winter ahead. Unpolluted waterways are essential for his health, his environment and the creatures who share it. If he survives to adulthood, he will play a critical role in a healthy ecosystem. He will build dams that cause streams to flood creating ponds and wetland areas. These areas created by the beaver provide needed habitat for a myriad of species including songbirds, waterfowl, fish, amphibians, aquatic animals…the list goes on. For now, he is just a little prince of the pond. "

KELLY DODGE (CANADA)

Agility. Speed. Velocity.
Snowshoe Hare
Oil on panel
8" x 16"

"Agility - the ability to change the body's position efficiently.

Speed - how fast an object is moving.

Velocity - the rate at which an object changes its position.

The Snowshoe Hare (Lepus americanus) is a rabbit-sized mammal that is named for its hind feet, which are large and well adapted for travelling across snowy ground.

The fur of the Snowshoe Hare is extremely thick and has one of the highest insulation values of all mammals. In winter, hares undergo shedding which transforms the hare's rusty brown summer coat into one that is pure white apart from the black-tipped ears and the feet, which remain grey."

TANIA DREELINCK
(BELGIUM)

Baby Caracal
Caracal kitten
Soft pastel on pastelmat
27" x 24"

"This little youngster could definitely be a superstar, being the embodiment of beauty, elegance, gracefulness, serenity and pureness. I was mesmerized by this little one's eyes and charisma.

In some continents, like in Asia, their population is decreased significantly. And in places like Namibia and South Africa these animals are officially signalled as problematical, which grants landowners the right to kill these beautiful creatures without a licence. "

TANIA DREELINCK (BELGIUM)

Chimp-and-See
The soul of a chimpanzee
Soft pastel on pastelmat
22" x 30"

"When meeting this beautiful chimpanzee, I was deeply touched by his soul. I wanted to bring this magnificent individual to the world, so other people could truly meet him as well, as the intelligent and very social being he is. Meet this beautiful male chimpanzee and look into his all-telling eyes...

Chimpanzee populations are endangered by the hunt for their meat, as well as by their disappearing habitats. 98% of their genes are common to those of the human race."

ROB DREYER (USA)

The Curious Chaparral
Roadrunner Chasing a Monarch Butterfly
Oil on canvas
12" x 36"

"When I was a child, every migratory season thousands of Monarch butterflies would blanket the bushes along the Mississippi River corridor where I lived. After a ten-fold drop in the population of the Monarch over the last decade, a 2016 study predicted an 11%–57% probability that this population will go extinct over the next 20 years. Milkweed plants are the only source of food for the Monarch caterpillar but these plants are rapidly disappearing, due to land development and the widespread use of herbicides. This depiction of a Monarch butterfly in a dry, barren environment, with a stalking predator, is a hint of this species' future without our intervention. Please plant milkweed. It's such a simple thing to do."

KIM DUFFEK (USA)

The Sun's Rays Penetrate the Night
Lesser Long-nosed Bats
Acrylic on gessoboard
12" x 16"

"The sun's rays penetrate the rock shelter that these female Lesser Long-nosed Bats (Leptonycteris yerbabuenae) take refuge in on their journey north to maternity roosts near the Arizona-Sonora border where they will have their young. They feed upon and pollinate columnar cacti and agaves, as well as eating the cactus fruit and spreading its seed on their long journey. Protection of their roosts and conservation of habitat containing columnar cacti and agaves along their migratory route are critical to maintaining this species. Wild tequila, mescal and bacanora agaves are bat pollinated, so drink to that!"

MICHAEL DUMAS
(CANADA)

Fox Sparrow Study
Fox Sparrow
Oil on Russian birch
20" x 16"

"I look forward to the arrival of fox sparrows early in the spring. They are particularly handsome to my eye, large for a sparrow, and decked out in bold patterns of rust and gray."

MICHAEL DUMAS (CANADA)

Innocence
Domestic dove
Oil on Russian birch
7" x 9"

"Upon stepping into one of the sheds where a friend of mine keeps his doves, I was immediately struck by one particular bird caught in the light from the window. Behind it, the interior of the shed seemed jet black to my eyes that had yet to adjust from the bright sunlight outside. The intricacies of straw and wood shavings made a wonderful contrast to the broader areas of white and black."

KATHLEEN DUNN
(USA)

The Sculptor
Pileated Woodpecker
Oil on board
36" x 16.25"

"Woodpeckers are the perfect bene-
factor of the practice of leaving old
trees on your property. The termites
and ants, found in trees as they decay,
are a major source of food for these
birds and their young. The tree in this
painting is a composite of three alders
I had photographed over the years,
one which was eventually whittled
and carved down to the ground. Nothing in nature is wasted."

KATHLEEN DUNN (USA)

Vintage
Steller's Jays
Oil on board
16.25" x 31"

"Every artist has that one painting that gets laid out, then put on the back burner in favor of other projects. This piece was one of those. It sat for 7 years before I felt confident that my skills in glazing and capturing that 'golden hour' light were ready to tackle the internal glow of these grape leaves. Even after doing the best job I felt I could, the piece didn't 'pop' until the blue of the fruit and birds was added, completing the analogous color palette."

KATHLEEN DUNPHY
(USA)

Up the Pass
Sonora Pass in the Sierra Nevada Mountains of California
Oil on linen
24" x 18"

"The Sierra Nevada mountains in Northern California take my breath away every time I travel up the pass to paint and explore. On a glorious autumn day, this scene stopped me in my tracks. As the sun edged towards the mountains, I painted studies and basked in the light and color of fall."

LINDA DUPUIS-ROSEN (USA)

Spotted Hyena at the Waterhole
African wildlife
Watercolor on canvas
16″ x 20″

"The hyena is the second largest carnivore in Africa. We watched this female and her four cubs play in a waterhole for hours. Any other animal that dared to drink at this waterhole was harassed by the older cubs. Hyena populations are currently on the decline due to persecution and habitat loss. Conservationists are working towards keeping them off the endangered list."

LINDA DUPUIS-ROSEN
(USA)

Painted Dog Pup of Botswana
Endangered African Wild Dog
Watercolor on canvas
16″ x 12″

"Painted Dogs, also known as African Wild Dogs, are among Africa's most endangered species. It is estimated that less than 7,000 remain in the wild. Conservation efforts, like Painted Dog Conservation (PDC) are working with local communities and are beginning to have a positive effect on the outlook of the Painted Dog species."

LYNN ERIKSON (CANADA)

Blue and Yellow Macaw
Bird
Acrylic on canvas
30″ x 40″

"Born and raised in British Columbia, I have explored the rugged nature and native wildlife of BC and the Alberta Rockies for many years. These experiences have greatly contributed to my vibrant watercolours and bold acrylics.

I have now begun a new series of tropical wildlife from the jungles of Central America. With this new inspiration I am taking an intimate look at the spectacular bird life there. My latest piece entitled ' Blue and Yellow Macaw' illustrates a close personal look at the character of this beautiful endangered bird. My hope is to share my experiences of the emotions and antics of these highly intelligent and cheeky birds."

LINDA FELTNER (USA)

Ladies First
Montezuma Quail and Harvester Ant
(*Cyrtonyx montezumae* and *Pogono-myrmex maricopa*)
Transparent watercolor
21" x 14.5"

"The courting call of Montezuma Quail is as inconspicuous as the bird itself. Descending whistles emanate from within grassy woodlands, announcing that spring has come to the mountain foothills of southeast Arizona. It's not easy to catch a glimpse of these elusive quail, either. Intricate markings of both sexes provide exquisite camouflage, creating the male's harlequin pattern and the female's delicate cloak of buff and umber. They do not readily flush when disturbed, but slip away into cover or crouch immobile until danger has passed. At dawn, the male keeps sentry as his lady sips from a rivulet."

JAMES FIORENTINO (USA)

Eastern Box Turtle
Eastern Box Turtle
Watercolor
22" x 30"

"I chose the Eastern Box Turtle as it is an endangered species in the State of New Jersey, although it ranges throughout the eastern United States. Their population in New Jersey is declining with habitat loss so to have them living on my property is quite the privilege. This original watercolor painting is part of a collection of artworks I have created with Conserve Wildlife on endangered and threatened species of New Jersey. The Eastern Box Turtle is such an incredible animal to paint with its unique shell and bright colors. The prehistoric look to turtles in general fascinates me and to show that detail and color in them is quite a challenge."

CYNTHIE FISHER (USA)

Vulterine Variations
Vulterine Guineafowl
Scratchboard
13″ x 20″

"These odd birds always make a statement; their colors and design on their feathers have to be seen to be believed. They reside in eastern Africa. Their natural color is a wonderful bright blue, but I thought it might be fun to explore a rainbow of possibilities in their plumage."

CYNTHIE FISHER (USA)

Family Ties
Burchell Zebra
Scratchboard
14" x 20"

"Zebras have to be one of my favorite subjects; they are an artistic delight! I've spent countless hours in Africa watching their behaviors, and I'm always struck by how much time they spend in contact with their family members. They are a very physical and 'touchy' species."

DAVID GALLUP & NANSI BIELANSKI (USA)

Jubilation
French Grunts, fish, coral
Oil on canvas
24" x 18"

"The first of a series of collaborative undersea paintings between Nansi Bielanski and me. This is a scene inspired by a shared experience diving in Belize. The slow motion of the fish, weaving among themselves as light danced through the school, left an indelible impression on us both."

MARTIN GATES (USA)

Morning Song
Crowing rooster
Holly (wood)
15″ x 8″ x 8″

"My favorite alarm clock! Holly is such a wonderful wood to carve; the color is perfect for almost any subject. I did take a mold from this carving and have a bronze edition available."

MARTIN GATES (USA)

Shadows and Moonlight
Owl and moon face
Bronze
10″ x 8″ x 8″

"This owl was molded from a woodcarving; the moon face and the owl are wonderful together."

FIONA GOULDING
(NEW ZEALAND)

Surrounded
Female Mallard
Oil on panel
12" x 16"

"A female mallard pauses in the clear water spying four fish which encircle her. Although mallards eat fish these are likely too large to interest her too much; she is content, for the moment, just to observe."

FIONA GOULDING (NEW ZEALAND)

Exposed
New Zealand Fairy Tern
Oil on panel
16" x 12"

"'Exposed' depicts the New Zealand Fairy Tern and the vulnerable nature of its nests. There are only about 45 individual fairy terns left in New Zealand, which includes only 12 breeding pairs. It is now confined to the lower half of Northland.

New Zealand fairy terns construct their nests on exposed, low-lying areas of shell-covered sand. The nest is a simple scrape in the sand. The exposed nature of these nests is one of the main reasons for their decline, being open to introduced predators such as rats, dogs, cats, hedgehogs and pests, such as humans. The nests are also vulnerable to being washed away by high tides, floods and storms. Beach activities can disturb nests and scare birds away from their nests, leaving the embryos to die from exposure. The birds' decline also results from the depletion of their sand dune habitat caused by residential development, the planting of pine plantations and pastoral farming."

PETER GRAY (SOUTH AFRICA)

Cat's View
Leopard
Oil on Belgium linen
35" x 53"

"Typically leopards and trees go together for a number of sound reasons such as escaping other predators, like lions and hyenas, and of course for hauling up a kill that can be eaten in comfort or stored for a meal later. Trees also make excellent vantage points for surprising potential prey or surveying their surroundings, hence the title, 'Cat's View'. This particular cat had pulled its kill up into the branches of an old, dead lead-wood tree and at this point was checking around for any possible threat and, of course, hoping for a stress-free meal. I chose not to place the bloodied kill hanging from the branches nearby but wanted to recreate the intensity of the moment and the agility of this phenomenal predator."

PATRICIA GRIFFIN
(USA)

Wrangler
Coyote
Oil on linen
60" x 20"

"The coyote's ability to adapt
and prosper is most admirable.
I watched this 'Wrangler' tiptoe
along the road, leap with precision,
and inhale its breakfast over and
over again."

**MARK HALLETT
(USA)**

Camarasaurus Pod by

Moonlight
Sauropod herd
Gouache, acrylic
24" x 18"

"This is the cover art I created for my forthcoming book, The Sauropod Dinosaurs: Life in the Age of Giants, Johns Hopkins University Press."

MARK HALLETT
(USA)

Into the Mesozoic World
Baby titansaurid sauropod
hatching
Gouache
24" x 18""

"This painting depicts a lion
cub size sauropod, Ampelosaurus atacis, and its sibling hatching in a nest of mosses and other vegetation in mid-Cretaceous northwest France."

SETSUO HAMANAKA (JAPAN)

Shishidome River
Reserved trout river
Oil on canvas
10" x 16"

"A trout river in a woods near Mt. Fuji. A rich water born in a deep forest runs 100km to Sagami Bay and the Pacific Ocean."

JULIA HARGREAVES
(CANADA)

Bird Bath
Juvenile Sharp-shinned Hawk
Acrylic
24" x 20"

"Not the usual pose for a hawk, but this one was taking a bath."

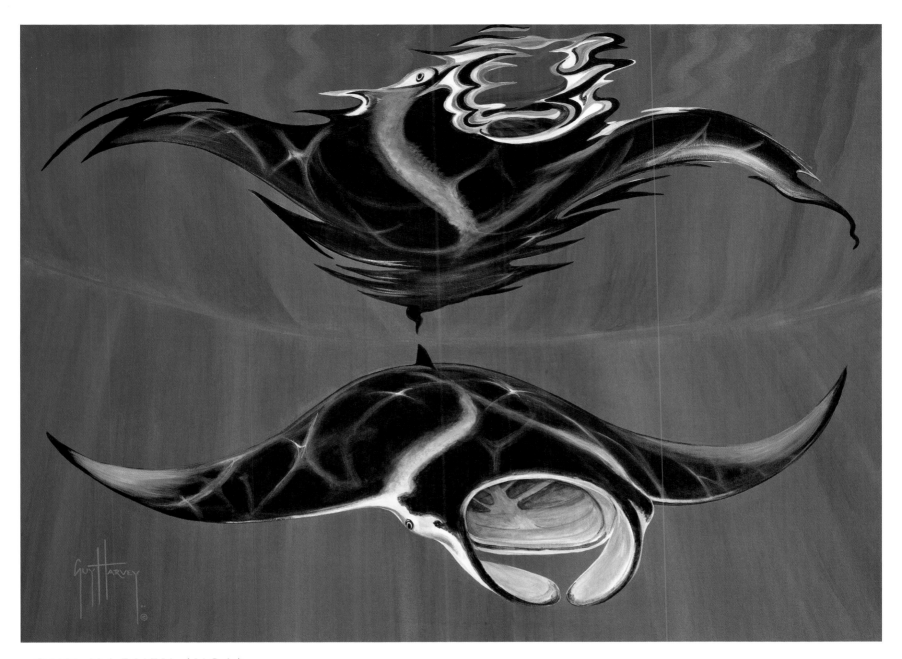

GUY HARVEY (USA)

Reflections Manta
Manta Ray
Acrylic on canvas
37" x 47"

KATHY HAYCOCK (CANADA)

A Special Place
Landscape
Oil on canvas
36" x 48"

"Carcajou Bay on Grand Lake, Algonquin Provincial Park in Ontario, Canada is both nearby and remote. Here is an area in one of Canada's most popular parks where it is still possible to be at one with the natural world and appreciate a spiritual connection while painting on site within the landscape."

JANET HEATON (USA)

A Sudden Departure
Domestic geese
Chalk pastel
29" x 40"

"'*A Sudden Departure*' became a painting after seeing the beautiful white geese on a lake in the Melborne Beach area of Florida. The white and orange color of the birds and their reflections in the blue water caught my eye as they began to lift off. Because of their weight, it took them time and distance creating a trail of foam and splash in the water. It was a challenge for me to paint and capture the motion and movement in the water which was necessary for both interest and contrast within the painting."

MARK HOBSON (CANADA)

First Sign Of Spring
Skunk Cabbage, Red-legged Frog, forest
Acrylic on canvas
30" x 36"

"The rainforests of the outer British Columbia coast are a wonderful tangle of abstract shapes created by moss-covered cedars, rotting logs and exuberant growth. The challenge is how to compose a piece that celebrates the feeling of this moody world within a rectangular canvas. I settled on a diagonal decaying log with a hint of warm light seeping through the background canopy. Set in March, the foreground centrepiece is provided by the fresh blooms of Skunk Cabbage (recently renamed Swamp Lanterns). These brilliant flowers look more likely at home in the tropics, but are always the first burst of spring growth in the dark, wet forests of the Pacific Coast. I'd been thinking of this work for years and finally just immersed myself in the joy of painting twisted cedar and dripping moss. Once the red-legged frog has finished laying its eggs it then returns to the forest for summer."

MARK HOBSON (CANADA)

Free Falling
Pacific Octopus
Acrylic on canvas
48" x 30"

"As a biology student at the University of Victoria I took a course in scuba diving. On the first dive we encountered an octopus with a diameter of approximately 12 feet. We followed this amazing creature for about ten minutes, and even in 40 years of diving, I have never seen one as large since. After a spurt of movement the streamlined shape would transform into a huge umbrella and drift slowly downwards, followed by another burst of smooth energy until it disappeared into the distance. I have painted several works inspired by this experience but this is the first octopus positioned in free fall as seen from slightly below. The kelp forests and density of life forms that fill every nook and cranny of the sub-tidal sea floor were very time consuming to paint but were a wonderful indulgence... almost as exciting as a 10-day dive."

JAMES HOUGH (AUSTRALIA)

All Together Now
Rainbow Bee Eaters
Acrylic on clayboard
13" x 24"

"The Rainbow Bee Eater is one of Australia's most remarkable and interesting birds. Behind the obvious beauty and striking features, lives a bird with more than one interesting habit. From a long distance a Rainbow Bee Eater can see its prey and swoop and capture insects, more often bees, before it lands on a nearby branch to wipe and squeeze the sting out. This bird constructs a nest in a chamber at the end of a tight tunnel it digs in the wall of an earthen bank."

JAMES HOUGH
(AUSTRALIA)

Tangled Hearts
Australian King Parrot
Acrylic on clayboard
24" x 18"

"One of Australia's most beautiful parrots, and one that every Australian recognizes, is the Australian King Parrot. The head of the male King Parrot is a striking red to orange. These parrots are found only along the eastern coast of Australia and within the heavy foliage of rainforests and woodlands. Seeds, fruits, nuts and berries make up the major part of their diet."

DEBBIE HUGHBANKS
(USA)

Prickly Perch
Sparrow on cactus
Acrylic on canvas
18" x 14"

"I am fascinated by the tenacity and determination of the tiny sparrows that are found throughout the United States. Sometimes they can be seen in the most unlikely places, such as perched amongst the beautiful blooms of a prickly pear cactus. I had to paint this tiny creature as it sat almost hidden and dwarfed amidst the colorful southwestern 'giants'.

Even though the sparrow is quite a common bird, it still needs to be cherished and respected, as does all wildlife around the world."

**TERRY ISAAC
(CANADA)**

Kicking Snow
Siberian Tiger
Acrylic on board
36" x 36"

"Siberian Tigers are one of the most beautiful cats on the planet. They are also one of the largest. Their beautiful pelts and habitat loss are the biggest contributors to their demise. I enjoyed painting this piece, creating the illusions of movement, and the patterns of the fur against the white snow."

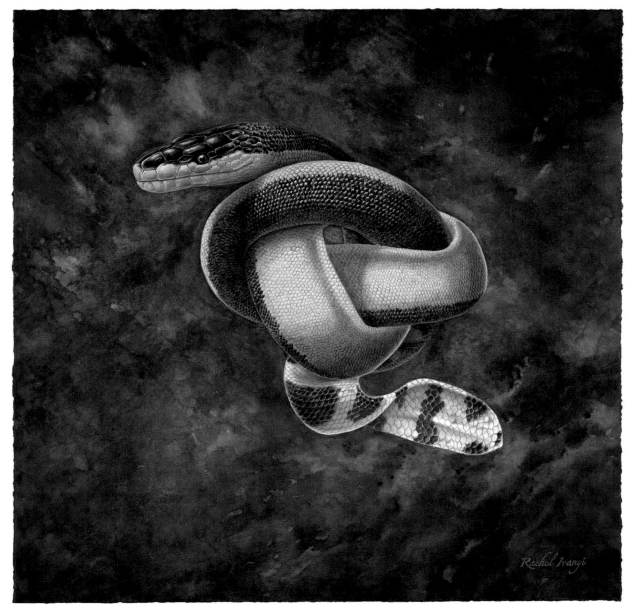

RACHEL IVANYI (USA)

Sailor's Knot
Yellow-bellied Sea Snake,
Hydrophis platura
Watercolor
35" x 35"

"The Yellow-bellied Sea Snake, *Hydrophis platura*, ties itself into a knot to shed its skin and rub off parasites. Amazed by this, I wondered about the remote possibility of it creating a specific sailor's knot. I used this visual metaphor to focus attention on the struggle between a fisherman's need to feed his family and protecting the inhabitants of our Sonoran Sea from unsustainable fishing practices. I created a life size clay model and, employing my father's trusty knot skills, tied it into a bowline, a popular sailing knot. After studying specimens at the local university, I turned my 'snake rope' into a muscled, scaled creature. I questioned my sanity on more than one occasion with this twisting and turning scale challenge. I felt it important to show how the knotted snake expands parts of its body, while simultaneously laterally compressing others, much like a folded ribbon."

PAT JACKMAN (USA)

Fox Den
Foxes
Colored pencil
27" x 33"

"The energy of these young foxes was amazing to watch, and quite a challenge to gather a still photo reference of them! I loved watching them play together and was inspired by their playfulness. The moss on the bark was beautiful, but took me the longest to draw. I think fur is much easier!"

KATE JENVEY (AUSTRALIA)

As the Sun Sets
African Wild Dog
Coloured pencil
10" x 12"

"As the sun sets on another day, a female African Wild Dog lounges content-edly just before the signal to begin the evening hunt, when she will spring into action, bound by the natural forces that co-ordinate the family group into such capable and proficient hunters. To watch these fascinating dogs in their natural environment is a truly rewarding experience."

KATE JENVEY (AUSTRALIA)

He Watches Over

Lion

Coloured pencil

10" x 10"

"A natural portrait of a lion. His story can be seen in the scars on his face and the courage that shows in his eyes."

STEPHEN JESIC
(AUSTRALIA)

Jewel of the Amazon
Scarlet Macaw
Acrylic on Baltic birch
24" x 20"

"Scarlet Macaws are considered the most magnificent bird of the parrot family. This Central American subspecies, called *Ara maco cyanoptera*, is native to humid evergreen lowland (up to 500 meters), subtropical rainforest, open woodlands, river edges and savannas of Central and South America. They usually nest in hollowed areas in trees, camouflaged and protected from predators by the thick foliage of the upper canopy of the rainforest. Scarlet Macaws were not endangered as of 2008, but the ever increasing destruction of the deep rainforest is threatening their habitats. Further contributing to their decrease in population is the spraying of pesticides by the companies selling bananas for export.

'Jewel of the Amazon' depicts a magnificent Scarlet Macaw preening itself. It is perched on a secluded branch in the upper canopy. The vibrant colours and contrast of the bird against the softness and misty atmospheric perspective of the rainforest was a sheer joy to paint."

MARY JANE JESSEN (CANADA)

Sentry Duty
Howler Monkey in Tortuguero Costa Rica
Oil paint on canvas
30" x 40"

"Everyday in Tortuguero National Park visitors are greeted with a sunrise and sunset vocalization of the adult male howler monkeys. This particular male is quietly watching the troop members feed and relax in the jungle canopy on the Anhinga Lodge grounds. Tortuguero's biological diversity is due to the existence of eleven different habitats including rainforests, mangrove forests, swamps, beaches and lagoons. Threats to this isolated area are illegal clear-cuts for banana plantations, and poachers who hunt the endangered marine turtles during the nesting season."

HANS KAPPEL
(GERMANY)

Sleeping Fennec
Fennec Fox
Oil on canvas
28" x 24"

"The tracks of this smallest of all canids had been the only proof of his presence that I found during a trip to Egypt and the Sinai Peninsula. Who knows where he was hiding? Perhaps he slept in a cave, and if so, what was he dreaming of?"

HANS KAPPEL (GERMANY)

At the Edge of the Field
Barn Swallows
Acrylic on canvas
22" x 31"

"Nearly everywhere in Germany industrial agriculture is destroying even the smallest remaining parts of our natural surroundings. Since we moved to a small village this has become an everyday experience for me. On my walks I am always happy if I find some 'forgotten places' where it is still possible to get an idea of what we have almost lost. This inspired me to paint 'At the Edge of a Field – Barn Swallows' and expresses my hope for preserving these areas for future generations to enjoy."

KARRYL (USA)

Pinnacle
Mountain Goat
Bronze
18.5" x 18" x 8.5"

"'Rocky Mountain High' is how I feel as I stand atop Mount Evans in the Colorado Rockies. At 14,271 Ft, it is a perfect place for me to observe the Mountain Goat. Their ability to navigate the rugged terrain amazes me. The Rockies provide important refuge for many dwellers of the high country such as the Mountain Goat, Rocky Mountain Bighorn Sheep, Marmots and Pikas. Unique fragile tundra vegetation lends to the wonderland of the peaks."

VALENTIN KATRANDZHIEV (BULGARIA)

The Red Princes of the South
Florida Flamingos
Acrylic on canvas
36" x 24"

"This piece was rendered after observing these beautiful birds at the National Zoo in Washington, D.C., April 2016. The National Zoo in-houses many species of birds which have been rescued after illness or injury. It was a pleasure to spend a few hours there observing the care that is given with the hope of returning the birds to the wild. The effort to protect and preserve the wildlife in our environment is of the utmost importance. Our survival depends on it!"

JAMES KIESOW (USA)

Balancing Act
Black-crowned Night Heron
Acrylic
16" x 20"

"I observed this night heron balancing on this cypress knee for over an hour, waiting for food to swim by."

MEGAN KISSINGER (USA)

The Beautiful Ones
White Ibis in Surf
Acrylic on gallery canvas
10" x 20"

"Not a day goes by in Florida that I can't find a few American White Ibis to paint. It's magical to see large flocks of them with their bright feathers shining as they forage along the aqua waters. Unfortunately, there have been recent studies that suggest the American ibis populations may again be on the decline. Runoff of sulfates into the dyked, straightened and dredged Lake Okeechobee and the Caloosahatchee and St. Lucie rivers creates havoc in the environment. Sulfates, over time, become methylmercury, an endocrine disruptor and neurotoxin that affect the courtship instincts of the birds resulting in fewer hatchlings. Rivers and creeks are the circulatory system of the Everglades. They flush billions of gallons of toxic water per day, eventually polluting the fisheries and coral reefs. The good news is that Floridians are working together, trying to restore the natural flow of the Everglades. Will we every solve our water woes in Florida? Only time will tell."

MEGAN KISSINGER (USA)

No Quarter
Laughing Gull Pair and Cormorant Thief
Acrylic on gallery canvas
16" x 30"

"On a trip to the Florida Keys, my husband and I watched a pair of Laughing Gulls defending their nest from a determined Double-crested Cormorant. It was trying to steal their nesting material to build its own nest, a common behavior for this species. The gulls were snapping and squawking and the cormorant would snap back at them and hiss. Neither side wanted to give up and the fight got pretty harsh. That's why I named this piece 'No Quarter'. If you don't know the term, you've never been a pirate!"

DAVID KITLER
(CANADA)

Piece Keepers
Embera Girl and Panama Rainforest
Wildlife
Acrylic on Baltic birch
25" x 33"

"'Our children are our future' were words from a conversation I had with the teacher in Llano Bonito – the Embera village where I was a guest, while studying the Harpy Eagle in the Darien region of Panama. I recorded them in my journal during AFC's first Flag Expedition, along with a question from my guide, who wondered if I knew what the children in the next village were doing in their spare time. It turns out that they were 'killing birds with sling shots'! With the image of this Embera girl, Midalia, I hope to make the visual connection between her and the responsibility her generation has to the environment with which they have been entrusted. Although this painting depicts wildlife from Panama's rainforest, from floor to canopy, the concept applies anywhere in the world. We are all pieces of the larger picture, connected to and responsible for each other. Our actions have far-reaching consequences – positive or negative."

97

DAVID KITLER (CANADA)

Backyard Encounters
Bee
Graphite & acrylic on Baltic birch
25" x 10.5"

"If I asked you to 'think of bees', it probably wouldn't take long before the word 'honey' came to mind. Four hives were recently set up on our rural property, and that's when my education began. On colder days I wondered how my 'guests' were doing; when the blossoms fell off the trees I wondered whether they could wait until the next trees bloomed. Each event caused me to worry about their fate. Then I found out that bees are responsible for pollinating one out of every three bites of food we swallow, and for increasing crop yields by as much as 300%! So I started to think that they must be able to look after themselves, that is until I learned that bee populations, in general, are in trouble. Whether by predation, pesticides, or diseases, their numbers are declining. My small part may be to offer sanctuary to a couple of hundred thousand bees. It can't hurt to also highlight one bee in a painting, hopefully prompting the 'selfish species' to imagine a world without tomatoes, beans, carrots, or hundreds of other vegetables because, if nothing changes, that's the direction our world may be headed!"

JOSEPH KOENSGEN (CANADA)

Frozen Morning
Pileated Woodpecker
Acrylic
16" x 21"

"This scene is from Riding Mountain National Park, one of my favourite places to visit. There was a dense fog the night before that left a thick frost on everything the next morning. The landscape was quiet and frozen with very few sounds but those coming from the birds that stay for the harsh winter. The Pileated Woodpecker is large, about the size of a crow, and the bright red cap on its head is a contrast in this black and white landscape. They are loud birds and both their calls and heavy chopping into trees can be heard echoing through the forest. Not too often have I seen so much forest frozen under a frost like this, but it was surely a delight to see."

**JOSEPH KOENSGEN
(CANADA)**

Canadian Reflection
Canada Geese
Acrylic
12" x 16"

"When spring has arrived on the prairies, a familiar sound and sight is the return of Canada Geese. Often a point is made to say that I've seen my first goose of the season. If they are returning, then you know that winter is on its way out. I've always enjoyed still, reflective waters, and it was a perfect setting for this goose pair that, at the time, seemed to have just found a spot to raise the next generation."

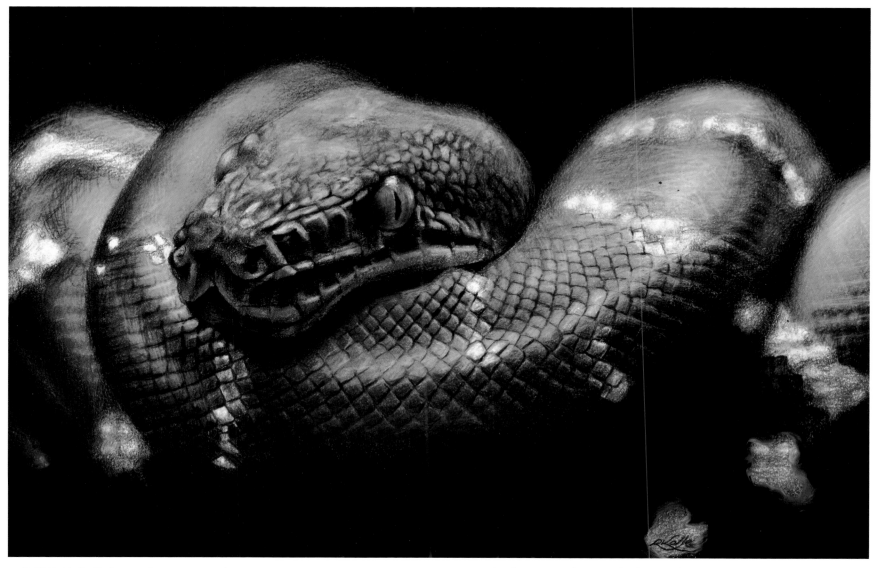

REBECCA KOLLER (AUSTRALIA)

Emerald Tree Boa
Emerald Tree Boa
Coloured pencil on paper
11" x 17"

"Appreciating the beauty of animals feared by many is one step toward the conservation of these creatures."

BARBARA KOPESCHNY (CANADA)

A Canadian Morning
Canada Geese, rock and waterscape
Acrylic on board
20" x 30"

"As the sight and sound of approaching geese lifts my gaze, I am reminded of the honour and privilege it is to regard nature, and in this moment my spirit flies above the landscape that surrounds me. A wondrous privilege and a moment to honour the beauty of ' A Canadian Morning'!"

BARBARA KOPESCHNY
(CANADA)

Shoreline Flight
Great Blue Heron, Rockscape
Acrylic on board
24" x 36"

"We share this world, its water, its rock, even the air and wind. To know this is the gift of wild places. But to witness this truth in such a moment is to experience the folds of time. An ancient reality overtook my paddle's quiet stroke that evening, touching me deeply - revealing the mysterious realm where the Great Blue Heron remains its fragile master."

KRISH KRISHNAN (USA)

Should I Trust You?
Brown Pelican in Tulum,
Mexico
Scratchboard
10" x 8"

"Somewhere in the ruins of Tulum, I came across this gigantic creature staring at me from such uncomfortably close quarters.

Probably more than five feet long, its wings flapped at a span wider than eight feet as it swooped upon a boulder at pecking distance. The graceful bird sized me up, its blue, beady eyes intently locked into mine. I froze, staying away from the reach of any art or photography paraphernalia lest I be maimed by his beak for my transgression.

After several long unrelenting moments, it let down its guard, allowing me to capture a few images digitally. The thrill of the moment was unforgettable.

I later learned that the Brown Pelican is really the smaller of the eight pelican species that inhabit our planet.

I enjoyed scratching its plumage with a #11 X-Acto blade, but found its elastic throat pouch the most challenging to scratch out!"

DEBORAH LAFOGG-DOCHERTY (USA)

Into the Light
Cape Griffon Vulture
Oil on canvas
28" x 24"

"My art combines two great loves: nature and painting. Most of what I paint is from life experience. While I am working in nature, I strive to give people a glimpse of how animals live in the wild, raise their young, court and survive. I appreciate the opportunity to enter into a secret world so many never get a chance to see and to provide a better understanding of the world we share.

My quest has been rewarding. My journeys have taken me from Everglades National Park to Denali National Park. Museum visits both at home and abroad have added to my development.

I share my passion for the world around us through color and excitement, which I believe is contagious!"

KAREN LAURENCE-ROWE
(KENYA)

Upon a Desert Sand
Desert Oryx
Oil on canvas
24" x 24"

"This is almost an abstract painting. I did see and photograph a line of oryx crossing a dirt track as they came up from the river in Samburu National Park, Kenya, but the land wasn't as barren as this. It was dry and hot and the ground shimmered in the heat and each day I returned to my tent, I was thirsty and dehydrated. The complete exclusion of any vegetation in the painting wasn't a conscious decision, but interestingly, this area almost became a desert over the next few months until at last the rain came."

KAREN LAURENCE-ROWE
(KENYA)

First Move
African Lioness
Oil on canvas
27" x 38"

"A visit to Ngorongoro crater produced some marvellous photo and sketching opportunities. We watched the approach of a superb lioness who was keenly focussed on something in the distance behind us. Out of the bushes emerged another lioness and three cubs. Their interaction and obvious affection for each other was a joy to watch. With lion numbers dwindling so rapidly, I will treasure that moment as I wonder if I will see the end of the last lion in my lifetime."

B. K. Lawes

BRUCE LAWES (CANADA)

All Tucked In

Lynx

Oil on linen

13" x 20"

"This painting depicts a dozing Lynx which is a medium-sized cat with long ear tufts, flared facial ruff, and short, bobbed tail with a completely black tip. It has large paws that will act like snowshoes to more easily support him across deep snow. Lynx like to hunt and travel alone, and are slightly more active at night than day. They will often take a 'cat nap' during the day as seen in this painting."

BRUCE LAWES (CANADA)

Savannah Siesta
Leopard
Oil on linen
9" x 13"

"This painting depicts the African Leopard reclined comfortably in a tree. This is a common place for the leopard to seek refuge as well as to sleep after eating its meal in the safety of his high perch. Lions are his greatest fear and although lions have been known to tree climb, they generally do not bother to expend the energy."

PATSY LINDAMOOD
(USA)

Wistful Great Blue
Great Blue Heron
Pastel on ampersand pastelboard
24" x 18"

STEVEN LINGHAM (UK)

On the Rise
Bald Eagle
Oil on panel
16" x 36"

"One of the United States' conservation success stories, the majestic and symbolic Bald Eagle, is 'on the rise'."

JAN LUTZ (USA)

Hoatzins
Rainforest birds
Watercolor on paper
20" x 28"

"I was quite taken with the prehistoric appearance of these birds, with their blue faces and spiky crests, that we saw in the Peruvian jungle. In 2015, genetic research indicated that the Hoatzin is the last surviving member of a bird that branched off on its own 64 million years ago, shortly after the extinction event that killed the non-avian dinosaurs. (Wikipedia)"

PATRICIA MANSELL (CANADA)

Shoreline Chorus
Steller Sea Lions
Acrylic on canvas
30" x 45"

"One of the strengths of wildlife art is its ability to tell stories. In my paintings I try to bring out the individuality of each animal as it goes about its everyday life. I portray many endangered animals, hoping that bringing them to life in my art will raise awareness of how close we are to losing them."

PETE MARSHALL
(AUSTRALIA)

Sloth Bear
Sloth Bear
Pastel and colored pencil
24" x 17"

"These bears have long been the subject of subjugation and abuse with their captors training them to dance on their hind legs using a tether through the incredibly sensitive nasal septum. The dancing bears have been trained for entertainment of tourists, and easy revenue for their captors.

I visited the conservation project of Wildlife SOS in India which rescues and houses these somewhat shaggy, lumbering creatures, and I was struck by the professionalism and dedication of the venture under difficult and constrained conditions.

All the housed animals bore the scars of the nasal septum tethers and teeth extractions, but they were all well healed and the animals healthy and interactive."

CANDY MCMANIMAN (CANADA)

Late Afternoon
Plumed Whistling Ducks
Oil
20" x 28"

"In the late afternoon, near Brisbane, we watched the elegant and alert Plumed Whistling Ducks fly out to feed in nearby grasslands. The elongated plumes made them appear so dapper. It is gratifying to know that they have a stable population in their range."

VICKIE MCMILLAN (USA)

Nose to the Ground
White Rhino
Acrylic on board
40" x 60"

"I observed and photographed the white rhino during one of my many visits to South Africa. Back in my studio in Texas, I recreated this spectacular event capturing the white rhino in a dry and parched land. Hiding in the thick bush is another rhino searching for grass. The white rhino is larger than its cousin the black rhino; unlike the browsing black rhino, the white is a grazer. Both of Africa's rhinos are endangered species, with some subspecies having become extinct such as the Western Black Rhino."

VICKIE MCMILLAN (USA)

Bull's-eye
Waterbuck
Acrylic on board
36" x 48"

"I observed this waterbuck around a watering hole where it descended during the heat of the day. Waterbuck form small groups of mostly females and young with a dominant male and are never found far from water. These brownish-grey antelopes have a shaggy coat with a white ring on their throat and rump. Only the male waterbuck have long, forward-curved horns."

**JOHN MEGAHAN
(USA)**

Idaho Skies
Landscape from western Idaho
Oil
24" x 18"

"I grew up in Idaho. I didn't appreciate that landscape when I was young, but now I find the sagebrush steppe lands to be quite beautiful."

**BILLY-JACK MILLIGAN
(CANADA)**

Hagersville Farm
Barn and sparrow
Acrylic
13" x 20"

"You can always find an old barn when you're out for a drive in the country. This time of year adds to the aura of the broken, weathered boards that hold these 100-year-old barns together. This one was located near Hagersville, Ont. I couldn't resist painting one of these pieces of history."

BILLY-JACK MILLIGAN (CANADA)

Duke
Mixed breed
Sepia
10" x 10"

124

"Occasionally, painting with minimal colour is excitingly different. This dog, Duke, inspired another opportunity, allowing me to spend more time on the lighting and the contrasting areas, giving me the chance to focus in a slightly different but refreshing way."

MARTI MILLINGTON (USA)

What Was That?
Canada Lynx
Acrylic
14" x 18"

"Canada Lynx are larger than a Bobcat but not considered a big cat. The lynx is a North American mammal of the cat family, Felidae. With the recognized subspecies, it ranges across Canada and into Alaska as well as some parts of the northern United States. The Canada Lynx is protected under the Endangered Species Act as a threatened species. Declines of lynx in the lower 48 states were due to trapping and timber harvests that removed, changed and fragmented habitat. Today, timber harvest, recreation and their related activities are the threats to lynx habitat."

Our dearly loved Australian koalas are in grave danger of vanishing over most of their range. Governments don't seem capable or willing to truly instigate healthy ecosystem management to prevent their rapidly escalating decline. The problems are many but all caused by humans - land clearance and fragmentation, disease, overcrowding in relict habitats, cars and roads, dogs, guns, mismanagement (or total lack of management). Some biologists have suggested the problem is simply too big and too hard for governments to deal with so they do what they nearly always do.....stick their bureaucratic fingers in their ears and rock back and forth while humming quietly to themselves and protecting their shiny little arses.

Gorgeous and precious animals like this male koala from the Kennet River area of our southern coast are dying in bucket loads or being culled when suitable habitats are available in many other locations. Trouble seems to be nobody in government wants the responsibility. Time for normal people to take action to protect their own country and their own creatures? I hope so because I personally do not want to leave a biosphere destroyed by money and apathy for our children. I would much rather leave behind beautiful creatures in my art (this one is a charcoal engraving) to inspire people to go out and cherish what we still have left and to recreate a world of which we can be truly proud.

And if you think I am being overly dramatic, have a look at the pics of this koala's formerly healthy forest and you decide if you need to stir your politicians to action."

STEVE MORVELL (AUSTRALIA)

Our Dearly Loved Australian Koala
Koala in eucalypt
Charcoal engraving on board
26" x 21"

STEVE MORVELL (AUSTRALIA)

'A Question of Trust'
Feeding Gang Gang Cockatoos
Pastel on colourfix paper
19" x 15"

"Gang Gang Cockatoos are fairly common here in the Grampians National Park and I come across them when cycling most days. The first indication of their presence is usually a dry, squarking creak, kind of like the sound made by a cork being twisted in the neck of a Scotch whiskey bottle.

When on the move they can be quite difficult to observe, but once they are feeding you could possibly sit down next to them and have a quiet beer and they would not move away. In fact I have on occasion climbed up into the higher branches of a eucalypt to sit on the same limb and watch them feeding happily on the seed capsules.

Only the male has the racy-red, punk hairstyle shown clearly in this pastel painting. The female sports a much more subtle, barred apricot breast.

This male was feeding with his partner on the eucalypts in my mate's front yard not far from here. They were down at my head height and allowed me to approach within 3 metres. They showed no fear at all and eventually I left them in peace to continue their feed."

DIANNE MUNKITTRICK
(USA)

Hide & Seek
Grand Cayman Parrot
Oil
30" x 30"
128

"The Grand Cayman Parrot is a subspecies of the Cuban Amazon Parrot. It is restricted to Grand Cayman Island and human development and habitat loss have resulted in it being on the endangered species list. I had the opportunity to view these birds while visiting the island."

ROBIN MURRAY (USA)

Jumbo Valley - Us and Them
Wildlife
Oil
8" x 22"

"Who owns these vast lands, us or them? Should we distort the grandeur of one's dreams to protect the innocence of the wild? When does it become mandatory for us to step in as an advocate to save the native wildlife, who have no ability to protect themselves, from the greedy.

Jumbo Vally has been a sacred land to the Ktunaxa First Nation, and a vital Grizzly Bear corridor for many years past. It must remain the same to protect the Ktunaxa nation's religious freedom and maintain a healthy grizzly population."

CALVIN NICHOLLS
(CANADA)

Sheer Power
Bengal Tiger
Archival paper
15" x 20"

"Sheer power and cunning are no match for the market forces that feed the onslaught of commercial poaching. Conservation laws on paper depend on enforcement funding in practice. One cannot exist without the other, just as the tiger cannot survive without our help. Thank you for your interest in my paper sculpture artwork and for your help in conserving the wild spaces and wildlife of our world."

CALVIN NICHOLLS (CANADA)

Weebale - Crested Crane
Crested Crane
Archival paper
17" x 18"

"The Great Green Wall offers more than a stark contrast to the Sahara desert to the north. Stretching from one side of the continent to the other it provides a natural barrier to the advancing sands and the threat of desertification. Creative and determined actions such as this prompt a heart-felt and melodic thank you in the local language. 'Weebale'."

131

SOLVEIG NORDWALL (USA)

Just Passing By
Whale Shark
Color pencil and metallic color pencil
on paper
16" x 20"

"Whale sharks have such mesmerizing slow grace despite, or maybe because of their vast size, the largest verified at almost 13 m in length. Their patterns are unique to each, blued by the tropical oceans they filter through their enormous mouths as they cruise, feeding on plankton and fish. They are listed as vulnerable but are still hunted in parts of Asia.

Shark populations globally are in serious decline, with some species reporting losses of 89%. It is estimated that 100 million sharks are killed annually for their fins and other body parts.

For this piece, the challenge was choosing which segment to draw. I wanted to show both their size and beautiful patterns, as well as their gentle nature. This close-up is how I wish I could swim with one as it drifts past into the deeper blue, trailing silver fish."

DORSET NORWICH-YOUNG
(CANADA)

Northern Dancer
Landscape
Acrylic on canvas
18" x 72"

"I live in British Columbia, Canada. As I paint my home environment, I continue to marvel at the variance in the landscape throughout the province. Here in the south coastal region we have a more moderate climate with a gentler landform. The northern coastal section has extremes of wind, heavy rain and rugged shorelines necessitating a strong grip on the earth. To me these tenacious survivors such as my 'Northern Dancer' have a certain joie de vivre that captures my heart."

MARY LOUISE O'SULLIVAN (USA)

Great Egret Fishing in Surf
A Great Egret is wading in breaking waves for fish
Oil on linen canvas
20″ x 30″

"Great Egrets always seem delicate and somewhat fragile. I associated the determination of this egret with the scarcity of bait-fish a couple of years ago due to a colder and longer winter than usual. They usually choose the calmer lagoon water over the open surf."

RON ORLANDO (USA)

Double Trouble
Black Bear
Acrylic
26" x 19"

"Pennsylvania has one of the largest Black Bear populations in the US. It is always a delight seeing them in the woods around our house. I also enjoy using young animals to highlight the vulnerability of our natural environment."

RON ORLANDO (USA)

Red on Red
Northern Cardinal
Acrylic
9" x 12"

"The male cardinal is everyone's favorite and sumac in the fall is one of my favorites. It seemed like a perfect match."

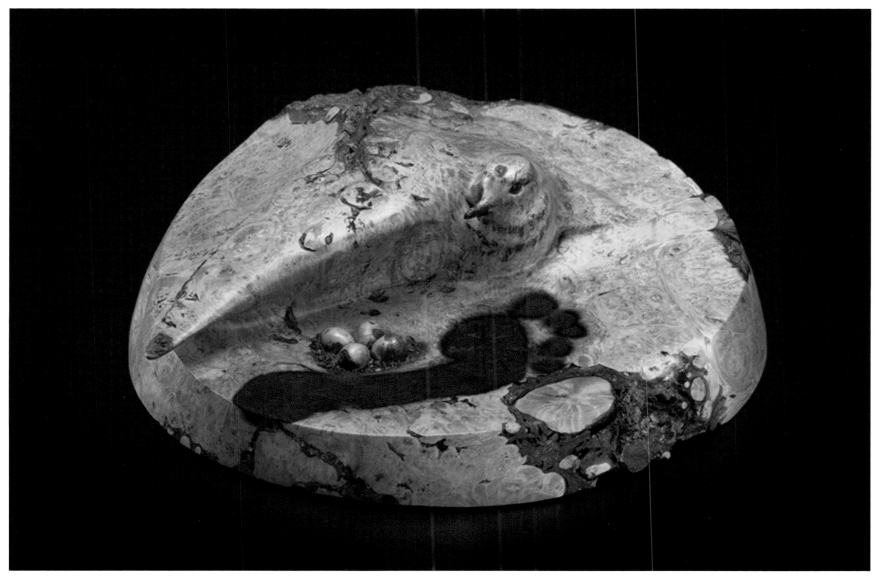

LEO OSBORNE (USA)

The Ploy
Killdeer and carbon footprint
Burlwood
6" x 16" x 16"

"Feigning my wing broken

To lure intruders away

They come greedily

Stumbling foolishly or unseen, unknown

But there

A dark presence

Leaving their careless footprint on our earth."

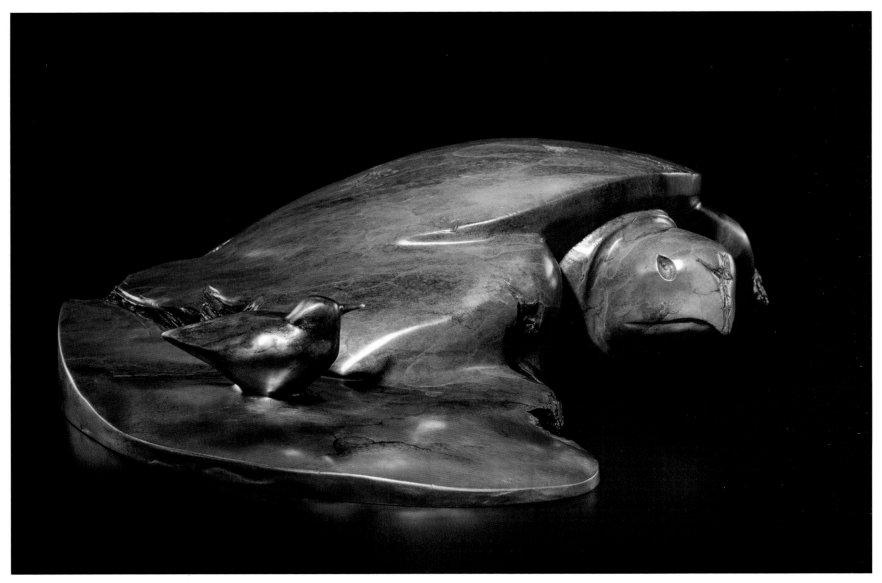

LEO OSBORNE (USA)

Return to Turtle Island
Sea Turtle and Shorebird
Bronze
6" x 26" x 19"

"Distant waters between you and me

With directions found in matrix energy

You flew above, I swam below

the mystic seas

Returning to turtle island

the place where our hearts wish to be."

VICTORIA PARSONS
(USA)

Visions
American Kestrel
Mixed medium - bronze & wood
35.5" x 22" x 16"

"I enjoy spotting and watching kestrels, the smallest of falcons here in North America. Here in the west I love watching these unique raptors hovering in the sky looking for prey as well as simply viewing them perched on telephone wires. I've chosen a preening pose cradled in ancient bristlecone pine using a contoured specimen of wood to complement the lines of this colorful raptor."

ANNE PEYTON (USA)

First Fall
Great Gray Owl
Acrylic
20" x 28"

"What a cool experience to see and hear a young Great Gray Owl. This September surprise encounter was in the Teton Mountains east of Driggs, Idaho, on the road to the Grand Targhee ski area. While Great Gray Owls are not endangered, logging and especially clear cutting continue to be a potential threat to these boreal owls."

ANNE PEYTON (USA)

Tanglewood
Gray Hawk
Acrylic
24" x 16"

"Southern Arizona is along the northern boundary of the handsome Gray Hawk. Not long ago, Gray Hawks were more common in the Arizona summer skies. Habitat degradation became a threat to them as cottonwoods, willows and mesquite trees along the few remaining desert riparian areas were either destroyed or died because of groundwater loss. Now that there are some improvements in protecting these habitats, the numbers of breeding Gray Hawks have improved for now, but conflicts over desert water will continue to exist."

MURRAY PHILLIPS (CANADA)

Simple Beauty III
Rushes at Cartwright Lake in the
Bugaboo Mountains
Acrylic
14" x 11"

"This is part of a series of paintings on seeing slowly and seeing the beauty around us - often hidden because of its simplicity and commonality."

POLLYANNA PICKERING
(UK)

River Wild

Tiger
Gouache on canvas
27" x 31"

"It is estimated that as few as 3,000 tigers remain in the wild. My charitable foundation has raised funds to buy equipment for Project Tiger rangers working in the field in India's National Parks to protect these beautiful big cats. While working with the Project Tiger rangers in Ranthambore National Park, I was able to observe and sketch this Bengal Tiger, cooling off in the water. Tigers are one of the few cats which actually enjoy swimming. Images of the paintings I completed following my expeditions have been distributed to schools in Indian villages as part of education packs to help teach future generations about the importance of preserving their unique wildlife."

POLLYANNA PICKERING (UK)

Highlander
Red Deer Stag
Gouache on canvas
22" x 27"

"Although I travel the world to study endangered species in their natural habitats, I also love to celebrate the wildlife of my native British Isles, including this magnificent red stag. The Red Deer is Britain's largest land mammal. Red Deer originally lived on the woodland edge, but the large scale reduction in tree cover in Britain over the centuries has forced them to adapt to life on the open hill. A herd of Red Deer live in the national park bordering my home in Derbyshire, occasionally straying into my garden."

RON PLAIZIER
(CANADA)

Interlude
Barred Owl
Acrylic
20" x 16"

"The Barred Owl makes his presence known with his call 'who cooks for yooouuu'! There's a family that lives in the bush around our house and it's beautiful lying in bed and hearing their call in the evening, but it's always a special treat and thrill when we get to see them up close in our backyard when they visit on occasion."

RON PLAIZIER (CANADA)

Trumpeter Swans

Trumpeter Swans
Acrylic
16" x 20"

"The Trumpeter Swan is a local favourite waterfowl here where they make the Crowe River one of their stops during their winter migration. They are the largest waterfowl native to North America with a wingspan that can exceed 10 ft. It's fantastic to see these birds up close, knowing that they are making a recovery after nearly facing extinction in the 1930's."

HEIDI PRATT (USA)

Disappearing Predator

Grey Wolf

Oil on canvas

24" x 36"

"This is an oil painting showing a ghostly image of a Grey Wolf depicting their struggle to survive. I'm trying to bring awareness and protection to the Grey Wolf through the compelling images of my art."

DAVID PRESCOTT (USA)

Bison Legend
North American Plains Bison
Acrylic/cotton canvas
32" x 32"
148

"The North American Bison is one of the true stories of conservation come back, I'm very glad to say. They are the essence of everything wild and free on the North American continent. Long shall they remain free to roam this great land."

JI QIU (AUSTRALIA)

Face to Face
Baby Plains Zebra and Red-billed Hornbill
Gouache and watercolor on paper
12" x 16"

"Zebras and Red-billed Hornbills are both black-and-white creatures living in Africa. This color is beautiful yet inconspicuous on the African savannah."

NATALIE RAFFIELD (USA)

Zebra Herd
African zebras during migration in Kenya
Acrylic on canvas
26" x 34"

"Preserving our natural heritage on Earth is, to me, becoming one of our fundamental issues for survival. Showcasing any natural environment and its inhabitants realistically with my paintings and photos is my main objective."

NATALIE RAFFIELD
(USA)

101 Zebras
African migratory zebras in Kenya
Acrylic on canvas
36" x 36"

"Preserving our natural heritage on Earth is, to me, becoming one of our fundamental issues for survival. Showcasing any natural environment and its inhabitants realistically with my paintings and photos is my main objective."

DAVID RANKIN (USA)

Tiger Shade
Tiger
Transparent watercolor
20" x 30"

About 3,000 wild tigers now survive compared with 100,000 at the turn of the 20th Century. Poaching has seriously impacted the probability of the tiger's survival in India. Kanha National Park & Tiger Reserve, located in Madhya Pradesh, was declared a forest reserve in 1879 and a wildlife sanctuary in 1933, and was part of the early Project Tiger efforts in the 1970s. Rudyard Kipling's famous Jungle Book was set in the forests of Kanha where bamboo flows into Sal forests and meadows and 22 species of mammals and 300 species of birds reside.

In the 1980s, on one of my early artistic expeditions to Kanha, I was inspired to do what I call "shade paintings" where I explore the complex shadows and shapes of subjects. This painting of a regal Bengal tiger resting in the cool shade of a Bamboo thicket grew out of one of those early experiences with tigers.

My hope is that in some way my artistic endeavors will inspire others to protect these beautiful animals and their natural habitats from utter extinction."

DAVID RANKIN
(USA)

Ranthambhore Ambush
Tiger and cheetal deer in
Ranthambhore (tiger sanctuary in India)
Transparent watercolor
20.5" x 28"

This painting represents the primordial "Predator & Prey" relationship of tigers and Chital Deer in one of my favorite tiger sanctuaries in India, Ranthambhore National Park. It is in Rajasthan, and was formally established as one of nine "Project Tiger" sanctuaries in the early 1970s. Ranthambhore's ancient fortress, situated 700 feet above the surrounding tiger forests, was built beginning in 944 AD. The national park is today considered to be one of the world's premier natural tiger habitats. Since the mid-1980s, I have been visiting Ranthambhore and many of my watercolors depict the diverse flora & fauna of this amazing reserve. A number of years ago the park's director at that time, Mr. Reddy, took me to his personal favorite vista overlooking the whole valley. During the ride he sat in the open jeep reciting aloud his favorite poem — *'Nature! We are surrounded by her, embraced by her, impossible to release ourselves from her and impossible to enter more deeply into her. She creates new forms; what has existed has never existed before, what has existed returns not again, everything is new yet again old. We live in her midst yet we are strange to her. She speaks constantly with us but betrays not her secrets to us. We are continually at work upon her, yet have no power over her. She is forever building, forever demolishing and her workshop is not to be found. She is the sole artist'.*

—Goethe in Fragments upon Nature

ANDREA RICH (USA)

Wood Ducks
Wood Ducks
Woodcut print
12" x 16"

"These colorful ducks are a favorite of mine and yet this is the first time I have done a print of them. I was hoping to find them in a setting that was as colorful in its own way, but without being too distracting. This slow moving waterway had a certain glow that attracted me."

ANDREA RICH (USA)

Pelicans at Big Sur
Brown Pelicans in landscape
Woodcut print
20" x 30"

"It was an early morning in winter on the Big Sur coast in California. The fog has thinned and is beginning to lift, but the sky is still gray as the pelicans cruise the cliffs, flying north in search of shoals of fish to breakfast upon."

REBECCA RICHMAN
(USA)

Home for Pygmy Nuthatch
Pygmies, communal songbirds, extended
family groups, viable, mature ponderosa
pine forests, healthy future.
Watercolor & pastel
29" x 20"

"Pygmy nuthatches are tiny, communal
songbirds that flit from branch to branch
with boundless happy energy. I've enjoyed
hours watching them and listening to their
cute 'rubber-ducky' calls. Pygmies breed
in large extended-family groups and need
mature pine forests to successfully nest.
During cold winters here in the west,
these little birds even roost together to stay
warm, being the very social creatures that
they are.

I paint the relationships in nature - the
space between the threads that weave
together the remarkable tapestry of biodiversity. In this painting, I highlight the
connection of mature forests to healthy
populations of songbirds. Fluid, viable
relationships bring into focus the connection of one life to another, and the intricate ways in which we impact our planet
and are impacted by it. My vision is that
people and nature can thrive together in
balance and harmony.

Pygmies, once common, face challenges
today in places like Colorado, where I
live, because of heavy land use alteration.
Let's keep our mature pine forests flourish-
ing to ensure that these adorable songbirds
have a bright, beautiful future!"

CRAIG ROBERTS (UK)

Youthful Exuberance
African Leopard cub - Botswana
Acrylic on gesso primed board
14" x 11"

"A beautiful leopard cub is excited by the kill hoisted in a tree by his mother."

VALERIE ROGERS
(CANADA)

Peregrine Falcon
Peregrine Falcon
Acrylic
12" x 24"

"When I paint, I am caught in wonder looking at the natural world. My paintings are my way of calling to you, saying 'this is wonderful, come look at this.'

Look at how beautiful this plant is, look at how intricate this spider web is and how wild and aloof the deer hiding in the woods are. Look at how the stripes on a chipmunk echo his shape as he dashes over lichen-covered rocks dappled with light.

Take a long moment to look at nature and see all the interconnected wondrous parts of it. That is what my paintings are - an in-depth study of what I experience outdoors. Our natural world is magnificent. My paintings are an expression of my appreciation for that beauty."

ROSETTA (USA)

Awakening Pride
Pride of lions on rocks, relief on back
Bronze
17" x 24" x 24"

"This pride of lions needs to wake up and get active after the long day's sleep. It's time to hide the cubs and head out for the evening's hunt, which is depicted in a relief on the back of the kopje (rocky outcropping in the Serengeti.) I watched such a scene once in Africa and was amused by the difficulty some members of the pride had in rousing certain sleepy-heads. I fear that it may be impossible to witness such a scene soon if the decline in lion populations due to habitat loss and human/animal conflict continues at the current pace."

LINDA ROSSIN (USA)

Fan Dancing
Wild Turkey
Acrylic on Strathmore Illustration Board 500
Series
3.25" x 5.25"

"There was a time when wild turkeys were pushed to near extinction by hunters, early settlers and habitat loss. This handsome bird is quite abundant today because of aggressive trapping methods, intense breeding programs and restocking efforts during the mid-20th century by state wildlife agencies. It can now be found in all of the lower 48 states, Hawaii, Mexico and southern Canada. Because of this astounding recovery, the wild turkey is a perfect example of what can be achieved when we join forces and work toward a common goal."

LEN RUSIN (USA)

Desert Sniper
Harris Hawk and Jackrabbit
Oil on board
16" x 20"

"A Harris Hawk swoops down on a young Jackrabbit as it tries to flee through the cactus of the dry desert region of the Grand Canyon. I witnessed this scene when I was the artist-in-residence in the Grand Canyon National Park several years ago. I was unable to capture the escapade with my camera, but tried to capture the same scene with my oil paints."

LEN RUSIN (USA)

Sleepers
Dunlins
Oil on board
14" x 17"

"Acadia National Park is home to many migrating shorebirds in the fall and spring seasons. I was fortunate several years ago to be the artist-in-residence in Acadia and was able to observe the shorebirds passing through. I was struck by how, during low tide with the morning mist, this group of napping dunlins was back-lit by the eastern morning light to create this relaxed mood of peacefulness. I tried to capture this mood on canvas with brush and paint."

162

ELEAZAR SAENZ (MEXICO)

Sweet Winds
African Lion
Oil on canvas
39" x 29"

"Is it the rain? Is it the distant murmurs? What is calling the attention of the predator? Perhaps it is the food that is moving on the horizon."

ELEAZAR SAENZ (MEXICO)

Desert Paper
Lagartija
Oil on canvas
23″ x 35″

SHARON K. SCHAFER (USA)

Breakfast of Champions

Loggerhead Shrike (*Lanius ludovicianus*), Joshua Tree (*Yucca brevifolia*), Pallid-winged Grasshopper (*Trimerotropis pallidipennis*),
Acrylic on hardboard

"The Loggerhead Shrike is a predatory passerine that hunts by day. Given the nickname 'butcherbird' for its carnivorous habits, it consumes primarily insects, but also is a fierce hunter of amphibians, lizards, small mammals, and small birds.

The powerful, hooked beak of the Loggerhead Shrike allows it to sever the neck of a small vertebrate. Due to the shrike's small size and weak talons, larger prey is often impaled on sharp thorns, yucca leaves or barbed wire where it can then feed on the anchored prey more easily. The shrike may also store its food impaled on a spine and return to its catch at a later time to feed.

Look for the unlucky Pallid-winged Grasshopper impaled on the Joshua Tree that is soon to provide the shrike with its early morning '*Breakfast of Champions*.'"

SHARON K. SCHAFER (USA)

Red-tail Sunrise
Red-tailed Hawk (*Buteo jamaicensis*),
Honey Mesquite (*Prosopis pubescent*),
Desert Mistletoe (*Phoradendron califor-nium*)
Acrylic on hardboard
30" x 24"

"Early in the morning, while walking through a favorite hidden canyon in the desert southwest, I heard the unforget-table hoarse, rasping cry of the Red-tailed Hawk, a 'kree-eee-ar… kree-eee-ar', a loud fierce scream beginning at a high pitch and slurring downward, perhaps a cry of annoyance or anger, in response to my appearance.

This hawk, soaring with wings in a slight dihedral, flapping as little as possible to conserve energy, circled above the desert floor, then finally descended to land in an old mesquite tree branch festooned with a few strands of dead desert mistletoe.

There the Red-tailed Hawk perched in the rising light…still and strong."

"I've always been thrilled to see a Steller's Jay; the blues are so inviting to an artist. There are a number of subspecies of this stunning bird found throughout Central America, North America, and Canada. I thought it would be appropriate to paint the Queen Charlotte Steller's Jay (*Cyanocitta stelleri carlottae*) among the poles found at Haida Gwaii (aka Queen Charlotte Islands) located on the north coast of British Columbia, Canada.

Parks and preserves are critical to conserving our natural and cultural heritage. While many of these key spots have been preserved as National Parks or other protected areas, it is still critical to manage all lands to maintain ecological health, and preserve critical cultural resources important to First Nations/Native American people. I chose to illustrate this Queen Charlotte Steller's Jay among the poles at Haida Gwaii to highlight the critical role these protected areas play for conservation of wildlife and cultural resources."

ROBERT SCHLENKER (USA)

Spirit Messenger
Steller's Jay
Oil on board
16" x 16"

NATHAN SCOTT
(CANADA)

The Chase
Salmon chasing herring
Bronze
24" x 16" x 23"

"I have spent the majority of my life living on the west coast of BC and I never like to pass up a chance to go fishing! As I reflect on the wonderful fishing trips I've had with family and friends, I'm amazed at the power, swiftness and versatility that salmon display while hunting. In this sculpture, 'The Chase,' I wanted to capture the fluidity and motion of the salmon in a chase."

SUZIE SEEREY-LESTER (USA)

African Parchment
White Pelicans
Acrylic on panel
16″ x 20″

"The dried mud leads your eye to the White Pelican nesting in the marsh. Tracks of some small creature are left behind in the parched sand."

JOHN SEEREY-LESTER (USA)

Defiance
Jaguar
Oil on linen
24" x 36"

"While traveling on the River of Doubt, Theodore Roosevelt and his son Kermit found the elusive jaguar."

JOHN SEEREY-LESTER (USA)

Finding Beshung
Giant Panda
Oil on linen
24" x 48"

"I had the opportunity to travel to China to see these beautiful animals in the wild in the early 90s, and have painted them ever since. They are a magical animal that I love to paint."

GERALDINE SIMMONS (AUSTRALIA)

Nocturnal Treasure
Owl Monkey
Scratchboard
6" x 6"

"Look into his eyes and what do you see? Wide-eyed, innocent and vulnerable, they have no voice except for the language they speak with their eyes. Owl monkeys are losing their forest habitat and numbers are declining due to the human footprint. New scientific research proves that protecting forests, even small fragments, is vital to the species' survival. If we lose them we lose a part of ourselves as well as the beauty and colour that makes our world. I chose the black and white medium to symbolize this."

172

KARIN SNOOTS (USA)

Free Bird
Surf of Atlantic Coastline and Sea Gull
Oil
16" x 40"

"The ocean waves gently break on the shoreline and the lone gull cries as he skims its contour. To some, these moments bring back cherished memories of times past. The seagull can bring to us a sense of friendship and community. Also, it can teach us how to ride the currents of the mental, emotional and physical worlds. But are we at greater risk that these natural occurrences are becoming insignificant, especially among our children? Personal interaction is quickly being replaced with static machines. Primary relationships are with machines rather then a multi-dimensional person. Personally, it's a great concern that technology is gaining such enormous popularity. We must work together to ensure that our oceans are restored so that future generations may enjoy the message of the seagull: to learn the many lessons of looking, living and being."

KARIN SNOOTS (USA)

Spirit of the Night
Great Horned Owl with night sky
Oil
12" x 36"

"In the night sky the silently flying owl, also called night eagle, can see that which others cannot. Is it a wonder that the owl in many cultures is a symbol for wisdom and guidance of the spirit? They are known to often bring messages through dreams, bringing a deep mystical wisdom and serving as a carrier of ancient knowledge. Can we call upon the owl to help us gain a deeper inner vision to uncover truth? Are we ready to integrate unwanted hidden aspects of our shadows into light? Currently there are some species of owls that are threatened at this point in time and may not be able to survive much longer. We can no longer ignore their fate just because we rarely see them due to their nocturnal nature. I have the personal experience of hearing the calls of the owl at night during spring courtship. The echo of their voice has a quality of peace and serenity hard to deny."

MORTEN SOLBERG (USA)

Waiting for the Fog to Lift
Gray Wolves
Watercolor
22" x 30"

"The Alpha female is watching for any movement through the fog while the male lies on a boulder in the background."

CINDY SORLEY-KEICHINGER (CANADA)

At the Temple
American Avocet
Acrylic on MDF board
18" x 24"

"In the early Spring, you see a lot of American Avocets with their pastel blue legs. They wade the shallows of the various sloughs, hunting for grubs and bugs. This scene, with the dead cattail reeds, looked like the bird was praying at a temple. So, the name. They are elegant birds and the colours all blended well."

PEGGY SOWDEN (CANADA)

Comforting Moment
Zebra mare and foal
Charcoal, watercolour
12" x 14"

"The protective gesture of the Plains Zebra mare toward her foal was caught in the afternoon warmth of the Serengeti Plain. In that moment it was easy to forget that habitat loss and hunting are still potential threats to this pair's survival."

EDWARD SPERA (CANADA)

Born to Run
American Mustangs
Acrylic on masonite
14" x 84"

EDWARD SPERA (CANADA)

Spirit Guide
Wolf
Acrylic on masonite
24" x 48"

JAMES STEWART (CANADA)

Sitting Bear
Bear
Bronze
7" x 5" x 5"

"After moving to Whistler, B.C., the influence of the environment has affected me deeply. It seems to seep into you over time. The bear is just one example of the creativity derived from living there."

LINDA SUTTON (USA)

To Be Determined
Polar Bear
Transparent watercolor
18″ x 29″

"The future is yet to be determined as he will have to be."

MARY TAYLOR (USA)

Libbie's Horse
Horse
Stainless steel rods, painted, clear-coated
78" x 80" x 33"

"I weld nature's creatures in mild and stainless steel to enhance our connection to and our understanding of the grand forces of nature and the movement and growth so inherent for our imaginations to flourish and reach out towards our dreams.

Over the last 40 years, I have constructed interior and exterior sculptures of wildlife. Employing steel rods, I render unique and intricate patterns of realistic animation with a strength of spirit and an intensity of aliveness. My sculpture is an announcement, a reminder and a heralding of our natural heritage.

This is a poignant, crucial time in the light of extinction. There are basic philosophical questions encompassing the juncture of life and death, beauty and harmony, of not only our endangered species but also of our own fragile selves."

MARY TAYLOR (USA)

Purple Gallinule
Purple Gallinule
Mild steel rods, painted
20″ x 11″ x 17″

COLETTE THERIAULT (CANADA)

Heartwarmer
Black-capped Chickadee and Trembling Aspen
Pastel
8.5" x 10.5"

"I am fortunate to live in the northern hemisphere where we can enjoy the wonders of the four seasons. As the days shorten near the end of summer, many birds prepare to migrate south. The resilient little chickadee, however, is a year-round resident and must face the harsh winter conditions that are fast approaching.

During fall, the landscape is transformed into a spectacular palette of oranges, reds, and yellows. The golden glow of the trembling aspen's heart-shaped leaves shining through the dimming evening light was something I always wanted to paint. Since chickadees are dear to the hearts of many, I felt he would make a suitable subject to incorporate in this scene."

MARTHA THOMPSON (USA)

More Than a Pile of Clams
Pacific Pygmy Octopus (*Paroctopus digueti*), Chocolata Clams (*Tivela planulata*), California Venus Clams (*Chione californiensis*)
Watercolor
7.5" x 12"

"In San Carlos, Sonora, Mexico, where we dive frequently, we used to find chocolata clams in abundance in certain bays. Over the years, hookah divers have eliminated that resource where we used to see them. Nowadays we seem to find them only far from populated areas. It happened in 2012, when we were traveling on our boat in the northern Gulf of California; we found a very pristine bay with lots of chocolata clams! We decided to dig up a few for dinner and as we were opening them, one of the clams was actually the home of a Pacific Pygmy Octopus! Pacific Pygmy Octopuses are known for inhabiting clam shells, old coke and beer bottles, etc. Intriguing and smart. Seeing an octopus on a dive or in an unexpected place is always a great experience."

JOSH TIESSEN (CANADA)

Defending the Paint
American Goldfinch
Oil on braced Baltic birch
20" x 32"

"At nine my brother and I fell in love with basketball, quickly moving up the ranks in city leagues, leading our teams to championship wins. But as short, white, Canadian kids, over time we realized our NBA dreams were unrealistic, so basketball gave way to art, but I still enjoy shooting hoops. For a few years I had the idea of painting an old basketball net with a bird perched on the rim, a sight I often see from my studio windows on the half-court in our backyard. I chose an American Goldfinch, whose striking yellow colour would complement the navy backboard square, and positioned him metaphorically guarding his key on a forgotten basketball court. While it's not too Canadian of me to have basketball as my favourite sport (instead of hockey) the game was actually invented by a Canadian, Dr. James Naismith, in Springfield, Massachusetts, over a century ago."

JOSH TIESSEN (CANADA)

Streams in the Wasteland: Whale Hymn
Humpback Whale
Oil on braced Baltic birch
36" x 48"

"As part of my '*Streams in the Wasteland*' series depicting wild animals in abandoned spaces, I imagined the concept for this painting over a year earlier, then found architectural reference from the ruins of a 12th century cathedral in London. This would provide an intriguing exterior for an ocean scene emanating through stained glass. I had become interested in humpback whales from watching the BBC series 'Ocean Giants', which recorded epic sights and sounds of the largest mammals to ever live on the planet. The behaviour of whales, specifically their vocalization, remains somewhat of a mystery to scientists. Many believe their 'songs' are more than mating calls, for the non-utilitarian act of expressing emotions. In contemplating this I recalled the gothic cathedral, a place for praise where parishioners sang hymns to their Creator. So also metaphorically the haunting chants from the giants of the deep bring honour to their Maker."

KIM TOFT (AUSTRALIA)

Coral Sea Dreaming
Coral reef at night
Hand painted silk
35" x 55"

"Coral reefs are one of the most threatened ecosystems on the planet. Coral bleaching and pollution are destroying healthy reefs and in turn, the animals living there are becoming vulnerable. This image is from my next children's book, 'Coral Sea Dreaming', which looks at the activity on the reef at night."

KIM TOFT (AUSTRALIA)

Flying Free in a Liquid Sky
Rays and sharks
Hand painted silk
35" x 55"

"The ocean has many mysterious creatures, and rays and sharks are two of the largest and most spectacular. I chose to paint them in silhouette to add a feeling of intrigue. This image is from my latest children's book, ' Coral Sea Dreaming' , which looks at the reef's activity at night."

JONATHAN TRUSS (UK)

Nowhere to Run

Tiger

Oil

32″ x 36″

Trying to find an original way to paint a tiger with a conservation message in the title was nearly as hard as actually painting it!"

JOYCE TRYGG (CANADA)

Sandhill Crane
Sandhill Crane
Watercolour on paper
16" x 22"

"The Sandhill Crane is in danger as the result of the loss and degradation of its habitat. The cranes preen with mud and vegetation stained with iron oxide and the resulting rust colour provides camouflage."

EVA VAN RIJN (USA)

Amazonians
Hoatzin couple sighted on upper Amazon, Peru
Oil on canvas
28" x 22"

"I had never heard of a Hoatzin until I saw this turkey-sized, amazing couple in a bamboo forest on the upper Amazon, one rainy morning. The Hoatzin has dinosaur-like claws on its wings, and it can swim. They nest near the river's edge in large groups."

EVA VAN RIJN (USA)

Sunbather
African Crowned Crane
Oil on canvas
24" x 16"

"On a cool morning in Tanzania, cranes spend their time getting into the sun's early rays and doing their preening ritual. In this painting I wanted to emphasize their grace and stature."

JERRY VENDITTI (USA)

Twilight Swan
Ornithology and Water
Oil on Belgian linen
12" x 18"

"Water is a precious resource and essential for life, but it is rapidly becoming contaminated and not potable. Because of this problem, I feel that all forms of living species on this planet will suffer if we do not rectify this plight."

© L.VIK

LYN VIK (CANADA)

All Sweetness and Light
Red Fox
Graphite and colored pencil
Acrylic
20" x 24"

"'*All Sweetness and Light*' is the representation of a beautiful vixen that lived on my acreage near Sherwood Park, Alberta. Each spring she had a litter of 4-5 kits and we often witnessed her instructing the kits in hunting and survival techniques. I spent many wonderful hours discreetly watching and photographing them play and tumble about. The reference photo used for this painting was taken on a frosty, sunlit winter morning along the border of a pond near her den. I was grateful for the opportunity to photograph her one last time before her sad disappearance shortly thereafter."

FRANK WALSH (USA)

Pt. Lobos Entourage
Humpback Whales and Bottlenose Dolphins
Acrylic
30" x 20"

"Pt. Lobos State Natural Preserve is part of the California State Park system. Located in Monterey, it has been called 'the greatest meeting between land and sea in the world'. The rugged shoreline is spectacular and those who have the opportunity to dive these waters are treated to a rich underwater preserve with a diversity of marine life."

FRANK WALSH (USA)

Morning Dew
Orcas
Acrylic
12" x 36"

"Just as the sun starts to burn away the morning fog, orcas rise with a powerful blow."

**YASUO WATANABE
(JAPAN)**

Migrans #02
Black Kite
Acrylic on paper board
29" x 40"

"A juvenile Black Kite is flying over a snowy mountain ridge. The figure appears to be golden in the deep silvery snow."

YASUO WATANABE (JAPAN)

Calliope #01
Siberian Rubythroat
Acrylic on paper board
14" x 20"

"The Siberian Rubythroat is a kind of thrush that breeds in Hokkaido, Japan.

The ruby color of the bird against the contrasting green of the background was very beautiful to me."

RICK WHEELER (USA)

Vernal Falls Moonlight
Vernal Falls, Yosemite National Park
Scratchboard/watercolor
20" x 12.5"

"An imagined full moon scene over Vernal Falls, Yosemite National Park, California. The U.S. National Park System is one of the great American success stories, featuring some of the world's most spectacular scenery for all to see, enjoy, and protect for future generations."

RICK WHEELER (USA)

Shadows & Light
Cougar
Scratchboard, watercolor, oil
11" x 14"

"The Cougar, or Mountain Lion, of the American southwest is an elusive and reclusive animal. Although primarily a nocturnal hunter, the cat is not opposed to daylight hunting, as well. Its tawny, reddish-brown coat helps conceal the animal in the rocky terrain of the desert southwest, making sightings rare and hard to identify."

JEFFREY WHITING (CANADA)

Saw-whet Owl Study
Saw-whet Owl
Bronze
10.5" x 5" x 5"

I've always been fascinated by owls as a whole, but particularly smitten with this little species, whose home spans much of North America. The Northern Saw-whet Owl (*Aegolius acadicus*) is arguably the cutest ambassador of the entire owl family. I've also always been intrigued by their incredible 'shape-shifting' abilities. Depending on the way it adjusts its plumage to reflect position, mood or attitude the tiny nocturnal raptor can appear almost like a completely different species. Though doing ok in much of its range, the darker plumed, Haida Gwaii saw-whet subspecies is threatened. As a bronze sculpture without accurate color representation, this study stands both for the species and for its Pacific northwest brethren who are specially reliant on dwindling old-growth forests with thick undergrowth. Loss of these forests and the introduction of Sitka Deer, which change the understory ecology, continue to impact the charismatic bird.

TERRY WOODALL
(USA)

Cleared for Landing
Canada Geese
Cedar driftwood
36" x 32" x 26"

"Natural driftwood forms wings and other features of these three geese in action. On the carved sections of the head and neck, dark stain contrasts with the light wood to highlight their markings."

ROBERT BATEMAN (CANADA)

Feast - Vultures
Eurasian Black Vulture and Griffon Vultures
Bronze
31″ x 20″ x 25″

Photo Credit: Birgit Bateman

AFC Festival Patron
Robert Bateman

AFC is proud to acknowledge Robert Bateman as Festival Patron for his generous support of the 2016 AFC exhibit and festival. Proceeds support AFC's art and environmental education programs.

Robert Bateman is recognized the world over for his exceptional masterpieces and for his dedication to conservation. His paintings reflect his caring nature and devotion to creatures big and small. Bateman has been instrumental in raising millions of dollars through the sale of his artwork for conservation organizations. Museums, galleries, royalty, and other avid collectors the world over treasure his artwork and admire his dedication to preserving and protecting nature's glory. Bateman's special commissions have included wedding gifts for HRH Prince Charles and HRH Prince William, a Platinum Polar Bear Coin Series for the Royal Canadian Mint, and an Endangered Species Postage Stamp Series from 1976-1981 for Canada Post. His major academic honors

include Doctorates in Fine Arts, Laws, and Science. Canada's highest civilian award, Officer of the Order of Canada, was bestowed upon him in 1984. The Queen's Jubilee Medal in 1977 and 2002 are also to his credit. In 1987 Bateman received the Governor General's Award for Conservation. Three schools in Canada now bear his name, along with a national award and major cultural institution - the Robert Bateman Art and Environmental Education Centre, in Victoria B.C. In 2008, Artists for Conservation acknowledged Bateman with its highest honor – the Simon Combes Award.

Recently, Robert's energies have been directed at the Robert Bateman Art and Environmental Education Centre - a unique facility based in Victoria BC, designed to host art exhibits, environmental educational programs, and his personal legacy of sketchbooks and paintings. Robert Bateman lives on Saltspring Island in British Columbia, Canada, with his wife, Birgit.

GUY COHELEACH (USA)

Indian Head Puma
Puma
Oil on canvas
24" x 36"

The Simon Combes
Conservation Award

2016 Recipient: Guy Coheleach

Internationally acclaimed artist, Guy Coheleach (pronounced Ko'-lee-ack) is a true master of the nature and wildlife art genres, and a lifelong patron of wildlife conservation causes. For nearly 50 years, Guy has channeled his talent to generating funds to support wildlife conservation around the world.

In 2016, AFC is recognizing Guy for a lifetime of conservation support, with its top honor: the Simon Combes Conservation Artist Award. AFC bestows this tribute annually to recognize artist members for their dedication to the conservation cause and outstanding artistic achievement. With the award, Guy joins a who's-who roster of international recipients chosen for their artistic excellence and lifetime of extraordinary support of conservation, including David Shepherd, Robert Bateman, John Banovich, Robert Glen, Sue Stolberger, Pollyanna Pickering, Dr. Guy Harvey, Richard Ellis, John and Suzie Seerey-Lester and Karen Laurence-Rowe.."

Guy Coheleach has donated his art for over 40 years to help many conservation causes since 1968. His Snowy Egret and Purple Gallinule print helped raise 13,000 new members for the Florida Audubon Society in the late 1960s. His "Endangered Species" and his 'Soaring American Eagle" original lithograph helped raise huge sums of money and memberships for the National Wildlife Federation and National Audubon Society respectively in the early 1970s. Guy recounted that in 1972 alone he raised over $172,000 in conservation donations, yet only the cost of paint and canvas were tax-deductible. In that time he has raised through auctions, hundreds of thousands of dollars for Game Conservation International, International Wildlife Conservation Society of Zambia and Safari Club International for over 35 years. In Tennessee his prints raised money for their zoo to buy a pair of Indian Lions and his endowment at the University of Tennessee provides numerous scholarships to the School of Wildlife Manage-

Previous page:Portrait of Guy Coheleach; Above-left: Coheleach with jaguar; Above-right: Coheleach painting amongst two young African elephants; Opposite-page (left): Guy facing a charging elephant during an early artistic research expedition to Africa; Opposite-page (right): SImon Combes Conservation Artist Award trophy designed by Peter Gray.

ment each year. In his many print and book signings a portion of the proceeds goes to local conservation organizations.

Guy Coheleach's paintings have received the Society of Animal Artists Award of Excellence eight times. He has also received the Artists for Conservation Foundation Medal of Excellence.

Coheleach has had 41 one-man exhibitions at museums in 23 cities from New York to Los Angeles from 1991 to 2011. The Carnegie Museum in Pittsburgh hosted his retrospective exhibition in 1995 and the Newark Museum hosted it in 1996. Along with over a hundred one-man commercial shows in various cities, his work has also been exhibited in the National Collection of Fine Art, The White House, The Corcoran Gallery, and the Royal Ontario Museum. Visiting Heads of State have received his American Eagle print, and he was the first Western artist to exhibit in Peking after World War II.

After serving as the 65th combat engineer's S-2 in Korea, Coheleach graduated from Cooper Union and received an Honorary Doctorate from William and Mary. He has been the subject of three films "Guy Coheleach and the Bald Eagle",

"Quest: An Artist and His Prey," and "Journeys of an Artist" by PBS in 2006. Additionally, he has also been the focus of articles in Reader's Digest, Saturday Evening Post, as well as numerous regional art and wildlife magazines. "The Big Cats: The Painting Of Guy Coheleach" by Abrams was a Book of the Month Club selection in 1982." Both it and his "Coheleach: Master Of The Wild" are out of print. "Guy Coheleach's Animal Art" by DDR Publishing is still available. Coheleach also wrote and published a book, "The African Lion As Maneater" in 2004 which has garnered rave reviews and was re-published as an iBook in 2016.

He received his first trip to Africa by winning a trip to London in the 1966 Winchester National Trap and Skeet Championships. Not content with skydiving and walking safaris, he takes his need for field experience to extreme. In 1972, he was run down by an elephant in Zambia. This hair-raising film has been on all three major networks. "This is exactly the kind of knowledge that has made him one of the best wild animal painters in the world admired by both scientist and art critics," says Pat Roberson in Sporting Classics.

A prominent member of AFC, Simon Combes was Project Director of the Kenya chapter of the Rhino Rescue Trust, an organization founded in 1985 to protect endangered species from being poached, and to help the communities surrounding Lake Nakuru National Park affected by wildlife conflicts. On December 12th, 2004, Simon was tragically killed by a charging Cape buffalo while hiking near his home in Kenya.

Simon was widely respected as a man of superb artistic talent, as a brilliant communicator, writer, instructor, world-traveler, painter, and as a steward of our planet. We were honoured to have him as a member of Artists for Conservation.

The award's trophy design was created by Peter Gray of South Africa and founded bronze with personal inscription.

About the Award

AFC's Simon Combes Conservation Award is the most prestigious award and highest honour AFC presents to an artist member who has shown artistic excellence and extraordinary contributions to the conservation cause, exemplifying the same qualities as the award's namesake. Nominees must have been a Signature Member of AFC for at least 3 years. Past honorees include David Shepherd, Robert Bateman, John Banovich, Robert Glen and Sue Stolberger, Dr. Guy Harvey, Pollyanna Pickering, Richard Ellis and John and Suzie Seerey-Lester.

WWW.DESERTMUSEUM.ORG

2016 Tour Premiere
Arizona-Sonora Desert Museum

The Arizona-Sonora Desert Museum is a combination of zoological park, botanical garden, nature education center, and conservation organization. True to its mission statement, the Museum seeks "...*to inspire people to live in harmony with the natural world by fostering love, appreciation, and understanding of the Sonoran Desert.*" To fulfill its mission the Museum displays living animals and plants in naturalistic habitat exhibits and stresses a strong interpretive and conservation focus on ecological processes.

The Museum is unusual in that it seeks to interpret in depth a limited ecosystem, the Sonoran Desert, located in Arizona, the northern Mexican State of Sonora, and Mexico's Baja California Peninsula. When applicable it interprets relationships with the desert's adjacent biomes, including nearby or enclosed mountain ranges, grasslands, the Gulf of California and its islands, and at its southern borders, thornscrub and tropical deciduous forests. The Desert Museum is regularly listed as one of the top ten zoological parks in the world because of its unique approach to interpreting the complete natural history of a single region. The Museum undertakes a wide and varied program to support its objectives of interpretation, education, research, and conservation.

The Art Institute began a series of art classes to expand students' understanding and appreciation of dessert ecology and conservation. As the artistic voice of the Arizona-Sonora Desert Museum, the Art Institute coordinates art classes, maintains the art collection and manages the many art exhibits that come to the museum. It is internationally recognized for offering a certificate program in nature illustration focused on the Sonoran Desert region. The mission of the Art Institute is conservation through art education which expresses the belief that students at the Art Institute develop a greater appreciation of the desert as a direct result of the time and effort they have taken to learn to draw its many aspects. Conservation begins with appreciation and understanding. The ties of observation and knowledge bind artists to conservation efforts. As John Muir said, "*When you tug on a single thing in nature, you find it attached to the rest of the world.*"

Top row: Gala night in the gallery (left); Esther Sample painting in Raptor Quick Sketch; Medal of Excellence winners, John Banovich, Frank Walsh and Terry Woodall (middle); Simon Combes Conservation Artist Award recipient Karen Laurence-Rowe (right); Middle row: AFC artist attendees to 2015 gala evening; Bottom row: View of lower "Spirit" gallery (left); AFC Festival Gala dinner performance with Calvin Dyck (right). Photos courtesy of Paul Moldovanos Photography.

2015 AFC Festival Recap

3 Weeks of Art & Environmental Events

Fairmont Waterfront Hotel & Grouse Mountain in Greater Vancouver, Canada

In September 2015, Artists for Conservation wrapped up its 5th annual festival - the longest and most ambitious one yet, spanning two major venues and three weekends and incorporating an Art Expo for the first time. The event welcomed public of all ages with a variety of interests - fine art, environment and conservation. It also brought together over forty AFC artists, a small army of dedicated volunteers, and supporters including RE/MAX, Deeley Harley Davidson Canada, our gracious hosts Fairmont Waterfront Hotel and Grouse Mountain and many other supporters and patrons.

The live exhibit featured 87 works, including 75 wall hangings and 12 sculptures representing 13 different countries. Many AFC artist members joined us for the opening of the three-week event and generously contributed their time to give presentations, lead workshops, and provide painting demonstrations. AFC's volunteers provided critical support over the ambitious schedule.

As part of the year's opening weekend in the heart of downtown Vancouver, eleven AFC Artists participated in a three-day Art Expo. John Banovich headlined as fea-

tured International Expo Artist and was joined by 11 others including Brent Cooke, Terry Isaac, Mary Jane Jessen, David Kitler, Kim Middleton, Murray Phillips, Esther Sample, Nathan Scott, James Stewart, Joyce Trygg, Terry Woodall and Jeff Whiting.

Renowned African artist and anti-poaching activist, Karen Laurence-Rowe travelled from her home in Kenya to receive AFC's highest honor - the Simon Combes Conservation Award.

2015 Festival Patron, Brent Cooke, featured his bronze sculpture "Silent and Serene" - a full-sized Great Blue Heron bronze sculpture with proceeds to benefit the Festival and youth education programs. Produced and delivered in association with AFC's annual exhibit, AFC's youth art and environmental education program – "Adventures in Art & Environment" – is designed to connect youth with nature through visual arts and build awareness around environmental guardianship. The program features a rich combination of inspiring indoor and outdoor activities designed to encourage youth to explore nature and species conservation. Activities include in-

221

Above-left: Grouse Mountain Skyride (photo courtesy of Grouse Mountain Resorts; Above-right: Squamish elder, William Nahannee at Grouse Mountain; Below: Painter-tainment body art "Wood Nymph" with AFC President Jeff Whiting (left); Pan flautist, Edgar Muenala (middle); Expo artist, David Kitler (right); Photos by Paul Moldovanos.

terpretive gallery tours, an eco-walk, documentary film screenings, First Nations cultural presentations, and a very special hands-on workshop with an AFC artist. The program is updated each year, so as to integrate conservation narratives touched on by artworks in the exhibit. Each year several schools in at-risk/ underserved areas, participate free of charge. AFC Artist Paula Wiegmink, originally from South Africa but now living in Australia, helped lead workshops over several days.

The Annual Gala Fundraiser was a beautiful evening to celebrate artistic excellence, our natural world and to honor those artists who have made an enormous commitment to conservation. This year Guy Combes returned to present the Simon Combes Conservation Award to fellow Kenyan artist Karen Laurence-Rowe. Awards of excellence were presented to Terry Woodall, Frank Walsh and John Banovich who were in attendance. Over 30 AFC artists attended the event from all

corners of the globe. Brent Cooke, this year's festival patron, gave a special speech addressing the unique relationship AFC as a charity has of bringing together two fields of study: the arts and sciences. Calvin Dyck and Betty Sunderman were the evening musical guests.

Bringing performance art to the stage at AFC's first Musical Celebration of Nature in Art local Vancouver musicians filled the gallery with art and nature inspired musical that was larger than life. Violist, Thomas Beckman performed a piece especially composed to accompany a slideshow of AFC Virtual Exhibit. Andrew Kim and Edgar Muenala brought the sounds of distant places with the sitar and pan flutes while Post Modern Camerata filled the gallery with a special rendition of Vivaldi's Gloria bringing the evening to a beautiful finale. It was an enjoyable evening for all who joined in the celebrations and came out to support AFC.

Above: Grouse Mountain overlooking Vancouver and Georgia Strait at sunset (Photo courtesy of Grouse Mountain Resorts); Below: Grinder, the Grizzly Bear (left); AFC Board Members Murray Phillips, Darcy Dobell, Brent Cooke and Jeffrey Whiting (middle); Violist Thomas Beckman (right). Photos by Paul Moldovanos.

About Grouse Mountain

Just 15 minutes from Vancouver's downtown core, Grouse Mountain is a vast alpine playground and Canada's premier four season destination. Grouse Mountain's iconic Red Sky-ride gives visitors and locals alike the opportunity to see the jaw-dropping majestic nature of British Columbia unfold in front of them during the eight minute ride from the Valley Station to the summit. Once at the Peak of Vancouver, visitors are greeted with endless experiences including Grizzly Bear viewing, eco-walks and ranger talks, 'hiwus' First Nations long house, world famous lumberjack shows, birds of prey flying demonstrations, Mountain-top Ziplining, five Mountain-top dining venues and the world's only wind turbine, aptly named the Eye of the Wind, with a 360 degree viewing pod which visitors ascend via a 55 second elevator ride

Grouse Mountain is a community leader with its education and wildlife conservation initiatives. The Refuge for Endangered Wildlife forms an integral part of this education platform and is a research and conservation centre at the top of Grouse Mountain that is dedicated to becoming a world leader in preserving both wildlife and flora at risk. The Refuge includes a five-acre mountaintop habitat that is home to two orphaned adult Grizzly bears and a spacious mountainside Grey Wolf habitat located at the base of the mountain.

To find out more about the AFC Festival, visit: www.artistsforconservation.com/festival
To find out more about Grouse Mountain, visit: www.grousemountain.com

 # *Artists for Conservation*

World's Leading Artist Group Supporting the Environment

Our Mission
To support wildlife and habitat conservation and environmental education through art that celebrates nature.

Our Vision
To inspire the world to cherish and protect nature by making conservation a core cultural value.

Who We Are

Artists for Conservation (AFC) is the world's leading group of artists dedicated to supporting the environment. Founded in 1997, AFC is based in Vancouver, Canada with a membership of 500 spanning five continents and twenty-seven countries. Comprising many of the world's most gifted nature and wildlife artists, AFC is a driving force in a global artistic and educational movement for conservation, inspiring individuals and organizations to preserve and sustain our natural heritage.

Our Objectives

- To provide powerful cultural experiences that inspire people to appreciate nature;

- To provide inspiring art and environmental education;

- To help the public understand how they can protect wildlife and wild places;

- To empower and support artists as ambassadors for the conservation movement;

- To connect art with science and catalyze synergistic conservation outreach projects;

- To foster fundraising opportunities for conservation with the art patron community;

- To support projects that heighten conservation awareness and provide a legacy of support for nature.

Artists for Conservation International Foundation is a Canadian-based registered charity (#860891761 RR 0001).

To donate, visit www.artistsforconservation.org/give

How We Do It - Key Programs

Artists for Conservation Annual Exhibit
AFC's annual juried exhibit celebrates the artistic excellence in the depiction of nature, raises awareness of conservation issues, and supports organizations dedicated to addressing them.

The Artists for Conservation Festival
Built around AFC's annual exhibit, this multi-day international art and environmental education event features workshops, demos, films, music, and special presentations.

ArtistsForConservation.org Website
ArtistsForConservation.org features thousands original and limited edition nature-inspired artworks for sale. It is the largest, and most visited site of its kind and a leading source for news and events.

AFC Flag Expeditions Program
This grant fellowship program connects artists with scientists in the field and supports exploration of the world's remaining true wildernesses and study of rare and endangered species.

AFC Marine Explorers Program
This program brings together teams of professional artists and leading subject matter experts in the field to study marine wildlife and the issues that concern them.

Art for Conservation
AFC's Art for Conservation program provides an online venue for the sale of artwork with a portion of the proceeds earmarked by the artist to support conservation organizations of their choice.

Adventures in Art and Environment Youth Program
Designed to connect youth with nature through art, this program challenges conventional environmental education models through experiential learning.

Documentary Films
Storytelling is a powerful tool in education and increasing public awareness. AFC produces a documentary series titled "Portraits of the Planet" to carry its message to a wider audience.

Awards
AFC Awards exist to highlight excellence in conservation and art and to empower and reward passionate professional artists as effective ambassadors for the environment.

Symposia & Lectures
Using art as a cultural platform for dialogue and connecting diverse audiences, AFC hosts conservation symposia, with lectures, panel discussions featuring leading experts and organizations.

Why Support AFC?

We live during an extraordinary period in history. Most who read this may well see over one-third of Earth's species vanish, along with dozens of human cultural lines and languages. The challenge of climate change, loss of biodiversity, desertification, overpopulation, and deforestation - each on its own - stands to adversely affect us all. Together, these challenges represent symptoms of a global pattern of impact by humans on the web of life that supports us.

Many artists today are active participants in an important movement, channeling artistic talent toward addressing the challenge of achieving a sustainable future. At the forefront of this movement is AFC.

We're extremely proud of AFC's dedicated artist membership of nearly 500 artists who support the charity's core administration and infrastructure costs. Our festivals and public events are self-funding through sponsorship and earned revenue.

100% of donor dollars go directly to charitable programming that has a unique multiplier effect, fostering artistic leadership, public education and collaborative art-science field programming. Under AFC's Flag Expedition program, a grant of $5,000 supports an artist expedition that typically yields many times more value to a designated conservation cause, through years of in-kind support and directed fundraising campaigns for the benefit of related field conservation projects.

Support AFC today and become a Patron of the Arts AND the environment!

AFC Membership (2016)

Jodie Adams
Gaye Adams
Douglas Aja
Harold Allanson
Phillip Allder
Carol Alleman
Charles Allmond
Stephane Alsac
Tom Altenburg
Wayne Anderson
Brenda Angelstad
Rosemarie Christina Armstrong
Stuart Arnett
Stephen Ascough
Curtis Atwater
Del-Bourree Bach
Priscilla Baldwin
Sheila Ballantyne
Elena Ballarini
Anne Balogh
Patricia Banks
John Banovich
Anne Barron
Sarah Baselici
Robert Bateman
Birgit Bateman
Joy Kroeger Beckner
Suzanne Belair
Craig Arthur Benson
Sarah Bent
Eric Berg
William Berge
Sally M. Berner
Alejandro Bertolo
Linda Besse
Nansi Bielanski
Cindy Billingsley
Adam Binder
Lauren Bissell
Peter Blackwell

Deanna Boling
Kirsten Bomblies
Beatrice Bork
Barry Bowerman
Peta Boyce
Jeffrey Brailas
Lynn Branson
Varda Breger
Carel Brest van Kempen
Caroline Brooks
Hilde Aga Brun
Renata Bruynzeel
Linda Budge
Sergio Budicin
Diane E Burns
Rob Butler
Florence Cadène
Michelle Caitens
Clarence P. Cameron
Ray Carbone
Roy Carretta
Brenda Carter
Roger Casteleyn
Gloria Chadwick
Larry Chandler
Peggy Chapman
Wayne Chunat
Michele Clarkson
Elizabeth Cogley
Guy Coheleach
Simon Combes
Guy Combes
RoseMarie Condon
Carrie Cook
Brent Cooke
Bryan Coombes
Anne Corless
Reggie Correll
Julie Cross
Deborah Crossman
Anni Crouter

Becci Crowe
Dennis Curry
Christian Dache
Daniel Davis
Ilse de Villiers
Karyn deKramer
Leslie Delgyer
Sara Beth Desjardins
Sunita Dhairyam
Rachel Dillon
Tim Donovan
Ron Dotson
Tania Dreelinck
Rob Dreyer
Angela Drysdale
Kim Duffek
Michael Dumas
Kathleen Dunn
Kathleen Dunphy
Linda DuPuis-Rosen
Ray Easton
Theresa Eichler
Richard Ellis
Mary Erickson
Lynn Erikson
Susana Falconi
Linda Feltner
Vicki Ferguson
Del Filardi
Jeanne Filler Scott
James Fiorentino
Karen Fischbein
Cynthie Fisher
Susan T. Fisher
Lindsey Foggett
Nancy Fortunato
Dawie Jakobus Fourie
Sunny Franson
Phyllis Frazier
Sid Frissell
Chris Frolking

Cindy Ann Gage
David C. Gallup
Tykie Ganz
Sam Scalz Garcia Jr.
Martin Thomas Gates
Rick Geib
Deb Gengler-Copple
Robert Glen
Patrick R. Godin
Paula M. Golightly
Carrie Goller
Susie Gordon
Fiona Goulding
Norbert Gramer
Peter Clinton Gray
Patricia A. Griffin
Laura Grogan
Liu Guangda
Gemma Gylling
Hap Hagood
Mark Hallett
Setsuo Hamanaka
Lorna Hamilton
Thomas F. Hardcastle
Julia Hargreaves
Harlan
Linda Parsons
Judith Hartke
Daniela Hartl-Heisan
Guy Harvey
Kitty Harvill
Kathy M. Haycock
Karole Haycock Pittman
Janet Heaton
Kenneth Helgren
Francisco Hernandez
Linda Herzog
Russ Heselden
Linda Heslop
LaVerne Hill
Guy Hobbs

Mark A Hobson
Edward Hobson
Gary Hodges
Leanne Hodges
Mary Louise Holt
James Hough
Hazel Howie
Debbie Hughbanks
Mike Hughes
Karen Hultberg
Dorothea Hyde
Barry Ingham
Margaret Ingles
Terry Isaac
Rachel Ivanyi
Pat Jackman
Graham Jahme
Clinton Jammer
Jon Janosik
Brian Jarvi
Kate Jenvey
Stephen Jesic
Mary Jane Jessen
David Bruce Johnson
Jay J. Johnson
Kevin Johnson
Richard Jones
Jason Kamin
Hans Kappel
Karryl
Aleta Karstad
Valentin Katrandzhiev
James Kiesow
Laura Kingsbury
Leslie Kirchner
Megan Kissinger
David N. Kitler
Christine Knapp
Eriko Kobayashi
Joseph Koensgen
Rebecca Koller

Jack Koonce
Barbara Kopeschny
Robert Kray
Jeff Krete
Krish Krishnan
Karin Kruger
Deborah LaFogg-Docherty
Linda Dawn Lang
Yvette Lantz
Judy Larson
Amy Larson
Karen Latham
Rebecca Latham
Bonnie Latham
Karen Laurence-Rowe
Yves Laurent
Bruce K Lawes
C. Frederick Lawrenson
Susan Jane Lees
Denise Lemaster
Esther Lidstrom
Patsy Lindamood
Steven Lingham
John Lofgreen
Craig Lomas
Anne E. London
Vladimir Lopatin
Olena Lopatina
Emily Lozeron
Bo Lundwall
Jan Lutz
Harro Maass
Dorcas MacClintock
Barry Kent MacKay
Craig Magill
Patricia M. Mansell
Michelle Mara
Cindy L. Markowski
Pete Marshall
James Marsico
Lucy Martin
Terry Owen Mathews

Denis Mayer Jr.
Chris Maynard
Chris McClelland
Cathy McClelland
Michelle McCune
Gregory McHuron
Candy McManiman
Vickie McMillan
Larry McQueen
John W Megahan
Kim Middleton
Billy-Jack Milligan
Marti Millington
Deian Moore
Mae Moore
Jason Morgan
Steve Morvell
Zenaida Mott
Frans E Mulder
Dianne Munkittrick
Robin Murray
Linda Muttitt
Chris Navarro
Francoise Nesse
Marilyn Newmark
Calvin Nicholls
Alison Nicholls
Carole Niclasse
Kentaro Nishino
Arnold Nogy
Solveig Nordwall
Dorset Norwich-Young
Mary Louise O'Sullivan
Ron Orlando
Leo E. Osborne
Wendy Palmer
Michael Pape
Linda J. Parkinson
Victoria Parsons
Kathy R. Partridge
Jeremy David Paul
Patricia Pepin

Jan Perley
Marcia Perry
Dag Peterson
Anne Peyton
Murray Earl Phillips
Pollyanna Pickering
Sandra Place
Ron Plaizier
Kay Polito
Betsy Popp
Heidi Parmelee Pratt
David L. Prescott
Ji Qiu
Stephen Quinn
Ahsan Qureshi
Radoslav
Natalie Raffield
Don Rambadt
David Rankin
Gamini Ratnavira
Linda Raynolds
Parks Reece
Sonia Reid
Vicki Renn
Werner Rentsch
Diana Reuter-Twining
Andrea Rich
Rebecca Richman
Martin Ridley
Craig Roberts
Valerie Rogers
Rosetta
Linda Rossin
Len Rusin
Maria Ryan
Eleazar Saenz
Jonathan Sainsbury
Esther Sample
Laurence Saunois
Patricia Savage
Sharon K. Schafer
Bill Scheidt

Robert Schlenker
Nathan Scott
Suzie Seerey-Lester
John Seerey-Lester
Steve Shachter
J. Sharkey Thomas
Clare Shaughnessy
Kathleen Sheard
David Shepherd
Naomi Rita Siegmann
Herb Simeone
Geraldine Simmons
Alex D. Slingenberg
Josephine Anne Smith
Karin Snoots
Morten E. Solberg
Linda Sorensen
Cindy Sorley-Keichinger
Peggy Sowden
Leslie Spano
Edward Spera
Melanie Springbett
Susanne Staaf
Eva Stanley
Barry Stein
James Stewart
Dolfi Stoki
Sue Stolberger
Zel Stoltzfus
Uta R. Strelive
Ken Stroud
Judy Studwell
Mark Susinno
Edward Suthoff
Linda Sutton
Joseph D. Swaluk
Ramona Swift
Frederick Szatkowski
Yutaka Tamura
Mary Taylor
Chris Telque
Sandra Temple

Colette Theriault
Claude Thivierge
Chili Thom
Martha Thompson
Josh Tiessen
Kim Michelle Toft
Daniel C. Toledo
Jonathan Truss
Joyce Trygg
Eva Van Rijn
Margarethe Vanderpas
Jerry Venditti
Diane Versteeg
Lyn Vik
Christopher Walden
Linda Walker
Cheryl Walker
Frank Walsh
Robert Wand
Val Warner
Yasuo Watanabe
Peggy Watkins
Pat Watson
Allen Weidhaas
Kathryn Weisberg
Gregory Wellman
Rick Wheeler
Jan Wheeler
Taylor White
Kitty Whitehouse
Jeffrey Whiting
Derek Wicks
Paula Wiegmink
Patti Wilson
Ria Winters
Terry Woodall
Ellen Woodbury
Lionel Worrell
Wyland
Tricia Zimic
Sallie Ann Zydek

Sponsors

Artists for Conservation *festival*

AFC would like to express its gratitude to the following sponsors who have provided support for the 2016 Artists for Conservation Festival and art exhibit in Vancouver.

Title Sponsor

Host Sponsor ———————————————————— **Sponsors** ———

Joyce Trygg | BC Wildlife Federation Artist of the Year 2010

Public & Community Supporters

Media & Promotional Supporters

- Arabella Magazine
- Arts-BC.com
- Business in Vancouver

- CTV-BC
- North Shore News
- QMFM 103.5 Radio

- Vancouver Courier
- Vancouver's North Shore Tourism

In-Kind Supporters

- The Clayman (Photography)
- ISCAPE Internet

- Lonsdale Rentals
- Thinkmint Media

- Lonsdale Quay Hotel
- The Heliconia Press

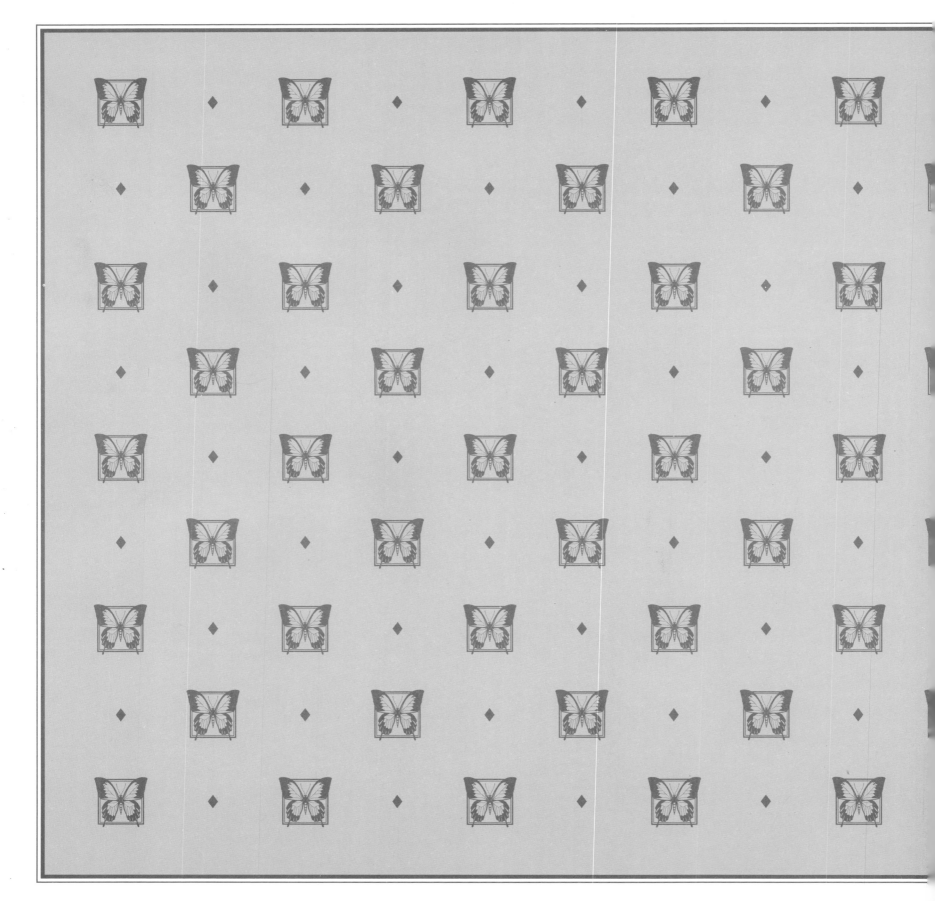